BECOMING A WHITE COLLAR TRADESMAN

BECOMING A WHITE COLLAR TRADESMAN

BROCK J GEBHARDT

PALMETTO
PUBLISHING
Charleston, SC
www.PalmettoPublishing.com

Paperback ISBN: 979-8-8229-4789-4
eBook ISBN: 979-8-8229-4790-0

CONTENTS

DEDICATION

I want to dedicate this book to America's tradesmen and blue-collar workers: all the men and women who have worked harder than anyone will ever know, the men who face the elements every day, risk life and limb to bring people's dreams to life, to drive progress and maintain infrastructure. These men are the backbone of America; if every tradesman walked off the job tomorrow, the results would be catastrophic—apocalyptic even. They keep the heat on, the refrigerator cold, the roof dry, the roads drivable, and so much more.

Secondly, I want to dedicate this book to my dad. He has taught me so much about work and the value of a blue-collar worker. He has worked his whole life as both a white-collar professional and a blue-collar small businessman. This dichotomy taught me a valuable lesson: you don't have to be typecast in a certain role; you don't have to fit the mold. He has spent his entire life working with his hands and educating children, bringing the wisdom of a hardworking, industrious, blue-collar man to the world of academia. Hundreds of kids over the years benefited from it, kids who were being told by every other teacher that they needed to go to college instead of following their passion for working on cars, welding, or carpentry. My dad was the voice of reason for many of these kids, a trusted role model who made it clear to kids that they could have a great life and provide value to themselves and everyone else in a blue-collar line of work. He continues to be a role model for me and my brother, and now our sons. He gave us permission through his leadership and example to follow our interests in the trades instead of demanding we go to college, and as a result, dozens of jobs have been created and our families live abundant lives. From your son, and all those whom you have positively influenced in your life, thank you, George.

AN INTRODUCTION TO CONSTRUCTION

If you have never worked in the construction industry before, there will be nuances and minutiae in this book that go over your head. But this book can and should still be a resource whether you're ready to take the step toward business ownership, moving up the ladder into that corner office, or waiting to start your first day of construction.

We all had to start somewhere. Every single man who has become a successful carpenter, electrician, plumber, or whatever started the same way. We all had to learn how to read a tape measure, swing a hammer, and sweep the floor in such a way that we don't receive an ass chewing.

Don't let starting from scratch stop you. The construction industry nationwide is in dire straits as far as recruitment goes. Many tradesmen are nearing retirement age, and there aren't nearly enough men to replace them. I have heard varying statistics on this phenomenon, but it's something like for every three men who leave the trades, one replaces them. What this means for you as someone who is interested in trade work is an unprecedented opportunity. There will be more millionaires made in the trades over the next decade than ever before in history. Even more common will be people earning well into the six-figure range. There has never been a better time to take the first step toward becoming a tradesman.

Unlike your teachers probably told you, if they were anything like mine, construction is anything but a dead-end job. I'm not sure what the purpose of this nefarious lie was, besides maybe propagandizing an entire generation into spending tens of thousands of dollars at state-run institutions, sometimes permanently indebting themselves, all for the profit of the government and the elite, but that's a story for a different book perhaps.

It's a narrative that has been around for decades. It wasn't always the case, but if you're reading this book, it was almost surely told to you during your education. I had an English teacher point out the window once and say, "You need to study, or you'll end up like that guy." He was pointing to a man in a hi-vis vest who was working on the street outside the school. That guy was likely outearning that arrogant, soft-handed little teacher, even as an entry-level worker on a road construction crew. Now the pay disparity is even more prevalent. Many of the so-called professional jobs, the white-collar jobs, are no longer paying what they used to; the market for those jobs is flooded, as everyone has a degree, so it no longer matters.

On the other hand, tradesmen are in high demand. The great ones can make millions, the good ones can make six figures, and the guys who can simply show up and do their jobs correctly will make $60–$80k easily. I am currently paying people with no experience $22.50 an hour to start at my company—no school, no training, no experience. Of the fourteen men I employ, several are six-figure earners, and a few others are close behind. Not one of them is an office worker; they all show up and get tool bags on and get to work. If that sounds like something you are interested in being a part of, there is an opportunity in every town and city across America to get paid a living wage and have someone teach you everything you need to know to be successful at a trade.

The construction industry is so hungry for good workers that if you can do the simple things that any job requires, or at least used to require, such as showing up on time and more than three days a week, you will have no problem holding down a job, even if you have zero experience. Another skill that will set you apart from the rest is the ability to deal with some physical discomfort. The trades often take place in less-than-ideal environments and conditions, and the ability to stay focused and push through being cold or hot, in uncomfortable positions, and dealing with cuts and bruises like a big boy will help you outperform the next guy. People get burned out quickly because the work can often be physically uncomfortable, so they leave for an easier job. People are also stuck in the mindset that construction is somehow a dead-end career. So they work in the industry for a couple of years and then jump ship to go back to college or take a job as a car salesman or some bullshit, as if that is somehow better.

If you work for the same company for five years and perform for them, you will likely find yourself in a company truck with a nice job title such as foreman or superintendent, making well above the median household income for your area, and with health benefits, a 401(k), and vacation time, just like the white-collar guy in the office down the street. But you will also have zero college debt and a skill set that is in extremely high demand in every corner of America. You could pick up and move today and throw a dart at the map; it's almost a guarantee that a decent job is waiting for you at that location. That all sounds pretty good, and that's the bottom of the totem pole when it comes to capitalizing on the opportunity that awaits in the construction industry and trades.

The construction industry has so much variety and so many different skill sets. It has something for everyone, and much of the experience is a transferable commodity. For instance, I can hire a guy with no siding experience but a year of framing experience and get him on track in a month; with someone with no experience at all, it might take six months or more. Same goes for guys switching from plumbing to HVAC or vice versa. Many of the concepts are the same, and understanding one trade or facet of construction makes you more valuable to all the others.

Even if you have no desire to be a business owner, or even an upper-level intrapreneur, I still strongly encourage you to consider taking that first step toward a career in the trades. It's a fulfilling and profitable line of work, and there is something to fit every personality, body type, and capability.

If you just read this and it sounds like you should give it a try, close this book, and put it away in a safe place. Go get a construction job and come back to this book in one year. At that time, the knowledge and lessons in the next pages will be of far more value to you, and you will be ready to start taking steps to an even brighter future.

THE PATHS TO PROSPERITY

The way I see it, there is one way to make millions in the trades: to own your own business—a business that can run without you for the most part, one that doesn't require your labor. You'll need employees and contractor cooperation, and it will take time, maybe a decade or more, to build it to the level at which it will be largely profitable. That's quite likely the only seven-figure idea available in the construction industry, or any industry for that matter.

There are two ways to make a six-figure income in the trades, and they both come much more easily than the full-fledged business.

The first is to become a highly effective intrapreneur, likely making six figures and enjoying benefits such as health insurance and retirement accounts. You'll be involved in the construction process but not wearing your tool bags. Or you may be the on-site superintendent, and you may wear your bags from day to day, but it's not your primary job; you are there to manage the project with a hands-on skill set and coordinate with the guy in the office. Both roles require years of experience in the trades to execute effectively. At one time, those office jobs were primarily held by people with college degrees and little to no actual industry experience. Now there is a shift toward promoting from within and hiring men and women who have been in the trenches, so to speak. A college education in construction management is great, but it's no match for someone who has spent those same four years or more on the ground at a construction site, learning the ins and outs of what managing a construction project actually looks like. It's far less to do with exact processes and spreadsheets than a college professor might tell you. It involves dealing with strong, conflicting personalities that need to work together and unpredictable schedules that are affected by everything from manpower and material shortages to the weather. An Excel spreadsheet has no power here.

The next way to reach that six-figure mark and likely the only other way to reach beyond the first $100k mark into the $250k range is to become self-employed. It's not the same as business, but it's closer, and it sets you on the path toward the million-dollar machine.

This is the most common way guys reach the six-figure mark in the industry. You are still on the jobsite working as a carpenter or plumber or whatever, but at the end of the day, you get to take the whole check home, not just your wages. It's a great way to make a living, and it paid my bills for over a decade. This is where most tradesmen stop their ascent in the industry, and that is just fine. It's a great place to be, these guys work hard, and there is minimal administration work related to this type of business. You'll likely have a small payroll of two or three guys, some insurance to pay, and a little bit of work to do on tax prep, but that's pretty much it; in the end, it doesn't take a whole lot more of your time than working a regular job. You get much more freedom than someone working toward the $1 million– or $10 million–a–year business, at least at first. The self-employed contractors are the guys you see at the lake on the weekends with expensive trucks pulling expensive boats. Life is good when you make $150k a year or more and can just turn your phone the fuck off on Saturday.

Now that that is established, we can move into the processes to reach those levels. The process of being successful as a self-employed contractor and a true business owner are one and the same to a point, the point at which you must make the transition from being on the jobsite with your men to letting them operate without you. This book will cover them in tandem.

WHY IS THIS IMPORTANT?

I see a flailing culture, a culture of men who do the least amount required of them, often not even that. We are in desperate need of new leaders at the ground level. It can be you; it can be me; we can lead a team of men and give them the medium to bring their dreams to fruition. So I decided to try to take that first step.

Getting started is hard. It's the first barrier to one's success, and for most people, it's the last. It stops most people in their tracks and turns them around right back to the hamster wheel they claimed they wanted off. You won't be perfect when you start—not even good probably—but just take decisive action, and the path will unfold before you. Bear this in mind as you read this book: I felt like I had something to share, so I took a chance and got started. The first draft of this book was a dumpster fire. Perhaps it still is; that's for you to decide. Either way I chose to act, you can too.

The information and stories in this book are here to help you from the beginning of your career through the creation of a business that makes $1 million plus per year with ten employees. I feel that if more of us can reach these or similar goals, we can start to change our culture for the better. If I can get ten thousand men to read this book and one hundred of them achieve the stated goal, one thousand jobs will be created, one hundred families will be liberated from financial slavery, and our country will become that much stronger. I am inspired to act now because I see two generations of American men that are at a crucial crossroads. These young men, from eighteen to forty or so, have a decision to make. Either turn away the tide of apathy and victimhood that currently laps at the withered fortress walls of American greatness and rebuild our culture, or succumb to it, forever dooming themselves and their children to a life that is less than. Less than what it could have been, less than our fathers and grandfathers provided us. We can truly be the second coming of American greatness, a multigenerational agent for change and forward movement. First, an awakening must take place. We must look back at the things that got us to where we are today.

We have been sold to the lowest bidder, town after town has vanished because manufacturing jobs have moved overseas, some construction jobs have been devalued and filled by illegal immigrant labor, and much of the traditional industry that built America and the American dream has been erased, sent overseas, often to the ends of perpetuating suffering and slavery in those countries instead of providing honest and honorable livings for the men of America. All this for cheaper, more consumable goods and higher corporate profits.

We all know this to be true, yet there is a line out the door of young men signing up for college, and it's crickets for the construction company trying to hire workers.

These young men have been coached into believing that working with your hands is somehow an inferior way to make a living. They have been told to seek the easy route, the safe route, to a comfortable middle-class existence. That notion cuts to the very core of what America used to be. We used to seek not comfort but new frontiers in business; we sought innovation and greatness. Now we preach the merit of mediocrity. We tell young men to avoid hard labor and that you don't want to end up being a construction worker because you might get some dirt on you. Instead, you should saddle yourself with enormous debt to compete for a job that doesn't pay enough to warrant the investment and prepare for a life of watching other people have what you want.

I say fuck all that.

The opportunity that lies in the rebuilding of American infrastructure, solving America's housing shortage, and reinvigorating manufacturing is one of unprecedented scale and depth. There will be fortunes made, not only by guys in suits and ties, but also by guys who got dirty and worked hard like their grandfathers did. The revolution of the office worker is over. Those jobs are drying up, and many of them stand to be eliminated by AI and other rapidly evolving technologies far sooner than any in the blue-collar space. And this is all the while the blue-collar sector is experiencing explosive growth and massive personnel shortages. So put down the latte and the laptop, delete the pronouns from your bio, and go get some work gloves. Let's rebuild America.

CHAPTER 1

CREDENTIALS—WHY LISTEN TO ME?

Allow me to introduce myself. My name is Brock Gebhardt. I am a contractor in Helena, Montana. I grew up in Bozeman, Montana, a short drive from my current home by western standards. My wife, Sarah, is a real estate agent, and we have two beautiful children. We live on a small farm in a modest home. I own Silver Creek Exteriors Inc., which I started in 2019 and have grown to a seven-figure business with fourteen employees. SCE is a siding installation company; that's all we do, every day. We have become the industry standard in our area in five short years because of the systems and principles I will share with you in this book. Along with my brother, Cole Gebhardt, I am also co-owner of a custom home-building and investment company, Gebhardt Development LLC, a company that is well on its way to becoming a local industry leader too. In addition to all that, I have over fifteen years' experience in the construction industry and more than one hundred real estate transactions under my belt as a real estate agent and investor.

I am not rich; I don't own a $100 million or even a $10 million business. I have no desire to own a $100 million company. I do want to own a $10 million business, but beyond that I have no further ambitions in business, to be frank. That is likely to change as I close in on reaching my current goal, as it always does; that needle moves farther away the closer you get to reaching it, it seems.

I am very much a regular guy who wants to live a life of abundance and freedom. That's the reason I work. I don't have any wild passion for construction or entrepreneurship. I'm not insanely disciplined or exceptionally intelligent, nor do I possess any special talents. I have just worked diligently and consistently throughout my life and achieved above-average results. That's what a seven-figure business is: it's above average. It's not exceptional; it's not sexy; it's above average. It's better than most. I'm happy with that as long as it provides the life I want for me and my family and helps others succeed along the way.

I feel like so much of the self-help content created for men is based around these men with hyper exceptional results. Don't get me wrong; we should absolutely be looking to those men for guidance and inspiration because they are the best of the best. But many of us don't want to pay the hefty price for what they have created. Furthermore, not one of us can get there without first going from good to above average. It's the first step on a path to greatness, so no matter what your endgame is, you must go through the above-average stage first. I feel like this mentality in motivational content turns many of us off from it before we even start; it all seems like too much.

I often listen to a podcast by Andy Frisella—you may recognize the name. He is a massively successful business owner, makes huge amounts of money, and provides jobs for thousands of people. He is also incredibly generous with his time and knowledge of business, having helped millions of people better themselves and grow their businesses—me being one of them.

That is incredible, and I have massive respect for that and for him, but I don't want that.

What I want is to provide jobs for fifteen to thirty people, operate an eight-figure business, and be able to pay myself $1 million per year. That is all I need and all I feel obligated to do. Perhaps it is not enough for some, but that is where my threshold is—where I feel I am providing an appropriate amount of value to myself, my family, and my community.

Additionally, when you listen to and look at people like the Frisellas of the world, who are living so big and have so much going on, you can't help but think their lifestyle or level of success is out of reach for you, impossible to attain, at least initially. The fact is that it is out of reach for most of us—not because it can't be done, but because few of us want to do the work required or possess the pure drive that it takes to build an empire. Those guys are one in ten million individuals. Let's just start with being one in one hundred. I'm still advocating being better than the next guy, just taking it one step at a time. Once you have bested the first hundred men, then the next thousand men, you can look to being one in ten thousand, and so on.

When you are standing on a jobsite in ten inches of mud with your tool bags on, climbing ladders and pounding nails all day making $40k to $50k a year, it's difficult to bridge the gap in your mind from where you are to where someone making a $10 million or $100 million a year is, and it can be demoralizing. It's hard to take actionable advice from someone who spent more on dinner last night than your car is worth. I have experienced this exact situation myself, and I felt like there was a missing link, a bridge that helps men get over that initial obstacle of feeling that the life they want is impossible. I know for a fact that there are many more men wondering how to make $100k or $500k a year than there are men wondering how to make $100 million. While I'm told the principles are the same, it goes without saying that the path, the discipline, and sacrifice required to make $100 million is something that few of us wish to endure, plain and simple, me included. I'm sure some will see this mindset as limiting or bitch talk, but it's the reality from my perspective. Take it or leave it, and apply it how you see fit.

This is where I feel I can be of service. I am standing just on the other side of that first little bridge. The bridge that connects the muddy, cold, tired construction worker struggling to pay his rent to the world of success and financial security. I can help get you across this first obstacle, close the gap between making $40k–$50k per year and making $100k, then to $250k and beyond. I'm here right now telling you that there is dry ground and solid footing on this side of the bridge and that if you put one foot in front of the other, you will make it across to a better life for you and your family.

I'm on my way to that $10 million company, but before I got here, at gross revenues of seven figures, I didn't see how owning a $10 million company was even remotely possible. I was that cold, muddy construction worker with wet feet and frozen fingers—I know that life better than anyone. It's like a false summit on a mountain, or dark highway unfolding two hundred feet at a time. Now I can see clearly how to get to $10 million a year in sales, because I made it to the top of the first hill. Trust me—come across the bridge; it's worth it. You don't have to keep going even, but at least get here; from here you can have a real effect on your community and help others build their lives. You can become the bridge for the next ten men, and so on. Together we can strengthen our communities and country and provide jobs and opportunity.

MY STORY

When I was growing up, I wasn't sure what I wanted to do. I wasn't sure what I wanted out of life; few of us are when we are young. I was always drawn to blue-collar work because that was what I knew. My dad had a couple of side businesses in addition to being a full-time schoolteacher. He ran a small herd of cattle, a haying operation, and a small firewood operation. As soon as we were old enough to help in any capacity, we were out there working beside him, often to his detriment, I'm sure, as I'm now experiencing with my own small children and their "help." But he was determined to instill a strong work ethic and respect for work in both his sons. We would help in the woods clearing trails and packing logs once we were able, then the rest of the year on weekends and evenings, we would split and stack wood for delivery. We got cold, we got hot, and we got bumped and bruised. We learned the value of a dollar and the sweat it took to earn it. Looking back, it's interesting to me: I never really saw my dad as a teacher. That was something he did in a building far from home; it wasn't who he was to us kids. Instead, he was a rugged, strong, industrious, and mentally tough blue-collar worker. Not only did we see him in that light, but I know he sees himself that way as well. He never identified with the white-collar academia crowd that made up many of his colleagues; in his mind, he is as I described. This mindset reinforced the idea that blue-collar work was of higher value, intrinsically at least, if not monetarily. I learned tremendous respect for him and men like him.

I graduated high school in 2007 and took a job as a construction laborer for eleven dollars an hour at a post-frame building company in Bozeman. I went to work the day after I graduated. It was a major culture shock for me; I was a scrawny eighteen-year-old kid with mediocre social skills, and they shipped me out of town for the week with a crew of guys in their midtwenties and thirties, most of them rough around the edges, trailer park–dwelling felons. The first week I worked there, I got into a fistfight with two of the guys in the hotel room. They came back drunk from the bar at 1 a.m., an outing I wasn't invited on, and decided to try to hold me down on the bed and kick my ass for no reason. They were less than sneaky while planning their assault, so I was ready. I kicked one of them in the face as they approached me and got up to meet the other and started swinging. It all resolved when the foreman walked in and started laughing at the guy I had kicked, who was bleeding from both nostrils. He picked himself off the floor, and they all started laughing, and then they just went to bed, like it was no big deal. I thought, "What the fuck!" I lay there awake the rest of the night wondering what was next. I learned to grow up quick in that kind of environment. It was a formative experience for me, working on those traveling crews, away from home with no support from my parents or anyone I knew. It forced me to immerse myself in work, as the company I had to keep wasn't always pleasant. So it was easier to just work, talk about work, and go to sleep thinking about work. It's hard to create a social bond with men you have next to nothing in common with; you can only talk so long about going to jail and the nuances of different strains of marijuana before it's more comfortable to circle back to shop talk. I credit the lack of distraction of a personal life with helping me learn as quickly as I did during that time.

I worked there for a little over a year; by then I was a lead carpenter, making thirteen dollars an hour. But I enrolled in college in the fall of 2008, at the behest of my parents and societal pressures, not wanting to be a loser and all. I gave college a shot, sort of. By the first week of my second semester, I knew I was dropping out. I hated it. I couldn't keep listening to people who had never left the education system stand in front of me pontificating about how to get ready for the real world. How the fuck do they know? They live in a safe, manufactured reality inside a system where everything is theoretical. I had gotten a taste of the real world working that first year, and I wanted to go back. I liked creating things, building with my hands and my wits. I liked battling the elements, and there was an element of danger that was appealing to a young man.

I dropped out of school and went on to get my job back at the same company. I worked there for another year or so, and I had advanced to a foreman position. At twenty years old, I was running a crew of men who were all older than I was, sometimes twice my age. It was a crash course in leadership. I worked to improve my leadership skills and my carpentry skills, trying to systemize and streamline processes. I didn't have a lot of mentorships at that company, which both served me and held me back in varying ways.

In the spring of 2010, the Gallatin valley experienced a once-in-a-lifetime weather event, a massive, powerful hailstorm with baseball-sized hail and strong winds, damaging and destroying the exteriors of almost every home in Bozeman. I took this opportunity to strike out on my own as a contactor. There was work to be done on almost every home, and it was all paid for by insurance. I had built two small barns for people on the side by this point, and I was feeling confident I could make it on my own. I did for the most part, but I didn't have the understanding of the market I should've had, and it cost me. I was chronically underbidding jobs and basically making wages on my labor. It was paying the bills, but it wasn't sustainable.

Then an opportunity presented itself in late 2010 that would change the trajectory of my career, an opportunity that would set me on the course to learn everything I am sharing in this book. I joined another business as an independent contractor. I worked with that business for over seven years, and we grew the company and learned a tremendous amount along the way. Eventually we went our separate ways, and I struck out on my own to pursue a career as a realtor and real estate investor, eventually circling back to construction in 2019. We will revisit many of these stories and experiences throughout the book.

KNOWING YOUR INDUSTRY

When I first started out on my own, I knew nothing about the construction industry. I had held one construction job, and that was the entirety of my scope of knowledge. As far as I understood it, construction companies did as much of the work as they could possibly perform on each project and hired subcontractors to do the rest, but I had no concept of just how specialized you could get or that the entire new construction industry was dominated by trade specialists and trending more so that way every day. Instead, I had learned that one company would do the concrete, framing, siding, roofing, insulation, drywall even, and the subs would get the scraps. It wasn't until I started at Montana Exterior Specialists (MES) that I realized you could build a business on just one trade. I was blown away. It's cringeworthy to look back at how uneducated I was in the industry I had chosen.

Once I realized how the industry operated, I was much more optimistic about my future as a business owner and operator. I would need fewer tools, less equipment, and less knowledge to become a competitor in my field. I had wasted upward of a year not understanding this concept, not getting specialized and focused on one trade. You can imagine my sense of relief, realizing that I didn't have to learn five other trades and procure equipment and supplies for each of them. My path as a business owner seemed considerably less arduous once this concept was applied. It was far easier to get focused and get serious about it, as opposed to looking at it as something far off and hard to achieve.

When starting a business, be sure you understand the arena you are stepping into. Make sure you understand who gets hired for what and what the going rate is for each type of work. Learn what equipment is generally required for each trade that you are interested in and how much it costs. Can it be rented? Or do you have to purchase it outright?

And what is the market for your trade? Some people get into something so hyperspecialized that they neglect the fact that the market cannot support the volume of work they need to make a living. Doing this research on the front end will save countless hours and dollars trying to figure it out on the fly. Make sure you understand the regulations and requirements to enter that industry or trade; some have lots of red tape, others almost none. The carpentry side of the industry has little to no qualification requirements, at least in my area of the country. But plumbing and electrical, for instance, often require years of apprenticeship and education.

Do your homework on the industry in your specific area; searching broad statements on the internet will not serve you here. Go talk to people, go find out how many people have business licenses in the city that list your trade, or just hop on a job listing website and see who is in demand in your area. Walk right up to a general contractor or superintendent on a jobsite and ask what subcontractors are hard to find or if they have any need for the work you are planning to perform. You will get a feel pretty quickly for whether your services are needed in your area. This industry is largely based on word of mouth and business-to-business transactions; you won't find the information you need without standing in front of someone, talking to them, and asking questions. Ask a fellow tradesman in your space how much they get per square foot. Some will tell you to fuck right off, but others will gladly share. Call and ask for an estimate on your own house from a competitor who doesn't know you if you must, but find a way to figure it out. Be intentional about the trade you choose, make sure you are skilled at it, know it front to back—and make sure it is in demand in your area.

As a quick example, last year, my wife and I flew into Phoenix, Arizona, on our way to a vacation in Mexico. We rented a car and drove down to the border. On the way, I noticed that maybe one in one hundred homes had siding installed. Almost every home or building was some form of stucco or exterior insulation and finish system. Furthermore, most of the roofing was ceramic tiles of one design or another. It became apparent that if I were to move to Phoenix or the southwest in general, I would need to choose a new trade or certainly face going out of business. That could be easy to overlook. It would be easy to think I could take my trade anywhere and succeed just as I have in my home state, but a few hours of passive observation proved otherwise.

Specialization is key to managing startup costs and operating costs, but be cautious about overspecialization. If you are a drywall contractor, you should be able to perform all drywall-related services: hanging, tape, and texture, and maybe even interior painting, if you have the skills. If you are a painter and only a painter, you need to do exterior and interior, not one or the other. This not only increases the amount of billing that is available on each project, but it also will keep you working longer than the next guy when things get slow. Additionally, your clients will gain value from not having to schedule two or three different contractors to complete the drywall and painting.

What you shouldn't do is be a drywall hanger and concrete flatwork finisher. If the trades don't naturally complement one another and offer better and more convenient service, you shouldn't be doing them both unless you plan on starting a fully separate business for that trade. And that's its own can of worms as well; unless you are a high-level operator already (pro tip: you're surely not, since you are reading this book), I wouldn't recommend it. It's a recipe for disaster when you fragment your mind in two directions. Most of us have precious few resources when it comes to brainpower.

Bottom line, find a trade that is in demand. You might be the best timber framer in the world, building beautiful decorative trusses, post-and-beam assemblies, and decorative corbels on multimillion-dollar homes, but if everyone is building apartments and not custom homes, you're shit out of luck.

Once you have identified the trade you are pursuing, ensure you understand the value of that trade within your specific market area. You need to know what the going rate in your area is for whatever trade you choose; sometimes they vary wildly, even in close proximity. Bozeman is less than two hours' drive from Helena. In Bozeman, they get 50 percent more for some trades, and in Big Sky, another hour from Bozeman, you can get 200 percent more. It's simple supply and demand, and it's broken down into micro markets, so be certain you understand yours, or you're going to get laughed off with prices that are way over market or taken advantage of with prices that are under market. Be careful with always chasing the higher-priced market too. Big Sky is great, and you can make piles of money if you are willing to make the drive and fight the snow eight months out of the year, but it's also prone to a boom-and-bust cycle. Sometimes there is more work than can be done, and other times, not so much.

I recommend building a business where you live, in your community, one that employs men who are your neighbors. Make a point of keeping them home every night with their families, not on the road in some shit hotel room. It might not be possible at first, but the more stable an environment you can provide for your men, the better candidates you will get to come work for you. Learn to make a profit at the rate in your immediate area. It can be done, because someone else is already doing it—find out how.

CHAPTER 3

OPERATING CAPITAL

Operating capital, or lack thereof, is likely the number-one reason blue-collar businesses fail. There are a lot of reasons for this, which I'm sure an individual much smarter and more well versed in finances than I am could better explain. But from where I stand, these are some leading causes (and ways to mitigate them):

#1 YOUR FINANCIAL THERMOSTAT

You see money from a perspective based on the income your family experienced during your formative years with them. If your parents brought home $70k between them, you likely see money as scarce and difficult to obtain. If they brought home $250k between them, maybe not so much, and so on. That being established, many tradesmen are in their industry because of a family member or mentor who was a tradesman or worked within the blue-collar industries in some capacity. It's a rare occasion that a lawyer's son becomes a drywall contractor. Many people in the blue-collar industries earn modest livings. The median income for a journeyman carpenter in the United States is right around $50k per year, a plumber

$60k per year, and an electrician $65k per year. Those are fine salaries and can raise a family and make a life, but your kids don't grow up with a mindset of financial abundance. My dad earned an amount similar to this, and my mother's income was sporadic, so I know this firsthand. It plagued me early on in business.

When you grow up with a household income of $100,000 or less, you look at $1,000 as a significant amount of money. I'm not saying it isn't, but when you are running a business in which tools cost hundreds of dollars each and you must provide supplies or materials, $1,000 doesn't even get you through lunch on your second day. It is all too common to have unexpected expenses well over $1,000 arise when you are operating even the smallest of businesses. You can't get caught with your pants down when it comes to understanding the amount of resources it is legitimately going to take to run your business.

It's easy for someone who grew up thinking $1,000 is a lot of money to get caught in a situation in which they are short on funds in an emergency because they haven't thought through all the possibilities or unexpected expenses that may arise, or they thought $1,000 would surely be enough to solve those issues. It can be extremely difficult to overcome your deep-seated perception of how much money is enough in each scenario, but it is vitally important to do so when starting a business—or even just operating a household—to avoid un-necessary financial hardships. A lot of tradesmen have saved up $5,000 or $10,000 and thought they were ready to start their own business, and although it can be done, it's a hard road. These guys feel like it *should* only cost $10,000 to get started because that was more money than they've ever had before and it *seemed* like enough, based on no data whatsoever. They are the ones you hear at the bar complaining about how it's not fair, it shouldn't be so hard, and that this widget and that doohickey shouldn't cost so much. Yeah, well, it fucking does, and you should have known that before you went off half-cocked.

The very first thing you should do when addressing this is take your financial thermostat out of the equation as much as possible. Since you are now aware that it exists, it should be easy to identify with a little self-reflection. Once you feel like you understand where your thermostat is set, it's a little easier to work around it, or at least understand how it might influence your next step. The next step is to take an honest look at your current business, your household, or your future business and give a purely mathematical value to the amount of money it will take to run it. We are emotional creatures, so we stick emotion into lots of places it shouldn't be, money being one of them. Look at the facts of how much you are spending or will need to spend—not how much you *feel* it should cost, but *how much it actually costs*. If you don't know where to start, just look at the things other businesses in your specific trade have and need to do their jobs—basic hand tools, specialty tools, supplies, equipment, trailers, trucks, employees, whatever they have that costs money—and google how much each item costs, or just ask. You will likely need these things to identify which items or services are recurring and at what intervals and to identify what is consumable and what the general life expectancies of your tools are. Ask an insurance agent to provide a quote for you and your business and what that insurance quote will look like as you scale up; I promise it's going to get bigger. Get estimated costs from anyone you think may become a necessary part of your business. With all this, you can build a solid outline for the costs you will be responsible for throughout the month or year. When you start a new business, those first months can be tough, and if you weren't honest about the amount it would cost to operate your new venture, it will be over before you get the first paycheck.

#2 CONFUSING WAGES, PROFIT, AND CAPITAL

Our society is painfully financially illiterate, and I am not far ahead of the pack, to be frank. I have an incredible amount to learn regarding business and finance, and unfortunately, I have learned most of my lessons firsthand. People in this country spend money they don't have and plan to pay it back with money they don't have a plan to make. That pretty much sums it up, but I have a book to write, so let me elaborate.

The worst offenders of all are often blue-collar workers or tradesmen. I hear guys all the time talking about how they made X dollars on a project when I know damn well what it pays, and the number they are quoting is the entire contract price. You didn't make $10k on that project just because you got paid $10k; you made $3k, and that's only if you did it all right. But this escapes them. They are the ones asking to get paid the day before they finish the work so they can pay their workers. They seem to forget about the wages, taxes, fuel, nails, supplies, and insurance that must come out of that project's gross revenue to make the business run. Guys see their bank account has $100k in it and think, "Wow! I have $100k!" No, you have $100k today, but tomorrow you owe a $15k payroll, then payroll tax, then insurance, then supplies, then a truck will break down, and you'll miss a billing cycle because you were too busy with all this other shit, and bam, you have $11k in your bank account and payroll is due again—it's $15k, remember? Yep, you are fucked. Then your men don't get paid, they all quit, and you go back to working by yourself and start the whole process over again, never learning your lesson.

It sounds almost satirical, but it's an endless cycle for a staggering number of blue-collar business owners. When you start making money, there needs to be a system for where it goes and what it's allocated for. I will admit I have struggled with this concept over the years. I have played it fast and loose moving money around and leveraging it sometimes when I shouldn't have, and it almost always causes a bunch of un-necessary stress and anxiety. So plan to divvy up your gross income so that you have all your bases covered.

However you choose to do this, you need to break it into three categories:

1. Wages. Figure out what you owe your employees and the taxes and fees that will be levied on those wages, and immediately pull that off the top of your gross. If you have employees, you will need an accountant to manage payroll, so this information should be easy to find in the payroll report they provide you.

2. Your pay. You could put this in the wage column, but it's a separate thought process in my opinion. Decide on a fixed amount you will receive from your business to live on. Be honest about the amount you want but also what your current revenue can support, and do your best to stick to it. It's a bad habit to start taking distributions to cover personal expenses, and you'll quickly burn through your operating capital if you are not careful. It blurs the line between your money and the business's money.

3. Capital. This is the part that is hard for a lot of us to do. You need to allocate the rest of that gross income

to the business. It doesn't go into your pocket; it stays in the business so that you have a war chest for a rainy day or to expand the business with new equipment or marketing. It will vary from month to month and check to check, but it's vitally important that you diligently put this money away; too many of us spend this money like it's our own, when in reality we need it to operate our business. Pay cycles are sometimes long and unpredictable in the blue-collar industries. You must be prepared to go sixty days minimum without a paycheck of any kind while still meeting your obligations to your employees and vendors. I look at this money in two parts. One part is your operating capital; this number should always be in your business account, and it should reflect your total payroll per month, your total loans liabilities per month within the business, and at minimum a few thousand as a cushion over and above those figures. At minimum, you should have enough to run your business without taking in a single dollar for thirty days, but I would shoot for sixty days, if possible. Keep in mind this amount will change and grow as your business grows. The second part is the money the business has on hand to spend when it is time for new equipment, new ventures, or marketing. Separate this money in your mind if you have that discipline or separate accounts, but keep it separate. It doesn't do anyone any good to buy a new forklift this month and not be able to make payroll next month.

If you can do these things consistently and stay disciplined in managing the funds that come into your business, you will stand out from the crowd in prospective clients' eyes and in prospective employees'. People talk, and general contractors will hear that you are not always beating down the door to get paid, which is obnoxious and comes off desperate and unprofessional. Potential employees will hear that you always pay on time and your checks don't bounce, and you'll gain a reputation as a legitimate company.

It seems so simple, but many business owners—and self-employed contractors—fail at this, and it causes them problems every month. One of the best accounts you could have in my area pays like clockwork every month on the tenth. It's awesome; you can count on your money being there on that day. But I have spoken with numerous subcontractors who won't work for them because they are too slow to pay! Are you serious? They give up an opportunity at fifty-plus projects a year because they can't wait at most forty days to get paid. I set the hook on many other subcontractors who want to come work with us because I will pay them the day they finish a project. They are willing to take less money in the long run so they can keep the shell game going, a game they don't even know they are playing. If they were to stop for a minute and really evaluate their financial situation, they would see that they are either not making any money or are way ahead of their cash flow and need to do something to rein it in. Do everything in your power to not find yourself in that situation.

Do the work and create the discipline to build a respectable war chest of operating capital and set yourself apart from the rest of the pack.

CHAPTER 4

THE EXCLUSIVITY TRAP

Don't be lured in early by an exclusivity contract, even if it's just a handshake deal. It has few upsides.

When I was starting out in Helena, I had a well-known company approach me with a proposal: I do all their work, and only their work, and they promise to keep me busy if they don't have to worry about me going and getting other work on the schedule. It's a common offer if you are providing value to a business and they see that you are hungry for more. It makes sense for them; they basically have you at their beck and call, you are essentially an employee, and you are putting all your eggs in that basket. The hook is effective for people who need or seek job security, but they unknowingly often trade upward mobility for stability. Those two things have a yin and yang–type relationship.

I declined the offer but made it clear I would still happily take on all their work. I worked with them for several years, performing every one of their siding projects, before parting ways because of some conflicts surrounding this general contractor's behavior and quality of workmanship, which I no longer wanted to be a part of.

But bear in mind what I just said: I declined the offer but still ended up with every single one of their siding projects for a period of years, and then *I* chose to walk away. I did all those, and another contractor's projects, instead of being stuck waiting for that one contractor to get projects ready or doing things outside my area of expertise to fill my schedule, or simply being out of work for a week or two at a time.

The moment you make that exclusive deal, you cripple your businesses potential for growth, and your business is now slaved to the production and prosperity of whichever master you capitulated to. They will begin to play goalie to make sure you don't stray, giving you lots of consolation work while you wait for the promised projects. Your siding crew will get to frame a house, then maybe do a roof, all of which they are 50 percent as efficient at, costing you money while you wait for your sugar daddy to bestow the coveted siding project on you. You get the point. It's the same for any trade; you don't want to have your trim carpentry crew out doing a siding project or your roofers doing trim carpentry; they suck at it. I've seen it all regarding this type of bullshit con job. It inevitably blows up in everybody's faces and creates negative results all around. Each party begins to believe they are somehow indispensable, and that is a recipe for disaster.

Another glaring issue with this type of arrangement is that you will struggle to maintain an understanding of the labor rate for your market. You may get your desired price out of the gate, although almost every GC will try to negotiate a lower rate based on you getting all the work. Even if you get what you want, what about a year from now? Three years from now? Will they accept higher rates? Or will they demand you maintain pricing? Without some other clients to test the market on, how would you determine what the market tolerance is for higher pricing? You can't and you won't. You'll end up working for well below market value for a long time. Over the years as a general contractor, I have hired some subcontractors who do a decent job but are *well* below the market rate for several trades. They almost always were party to one of these agreements in the recent past. They decide to venture out and are selling their services for what they believe to be the going rate, but sometimes it's as low as 50 percent of the competition. They get the work of course, but it is months, maybe years before they figure out that they can get more for their work, sometimes at the cost of hundreds of thousands of dollars in missed opportunity. All because they took the low-hanging fruit with the first general contractor who got them to drink the Kool-Aid.

At Silver Creek Exteriors, we have successfully captured a large market share of the new construction cladding market in our area using the principle that we will do *all* your work, but not *only* your work. We perform 100 percent of the projects for four major home builders and general contractors, which in our market of roughly sixty thousand people accounts for a significant portion of the new construction starts in a given year.

We acquired them slowly as we grew our workforce and trained the necessary team members to produce the quality and production that we needed to stay on brand with every project. Once we had a team that could handle the work, I would reach out to the new prospective client, make my pitch, and secure the first job. By the time you are expanding to multiple larger clients, this should be an easy sell for the most part. You should have enough examples of work and positive word of mouth that they already know who you are and are at least somewhat familiar with your work and workmanship.

The first job is the most important moment of this new partnership. All expectations will be set: the quality, the pace, the billing rate, et cetera. Make sure that you are on point with every detail; your crew needs to be there when you said they would be, they need to keep the jobsite spotless, the quality of your workmanship needs to be second to none, and the pace needs to be full throttle. When you come in and knock their socks off on your first project, you have them. They will remember it, and if you stay on brand and produce results like that regularly, you won't suffer losing that client if your guys have an off week or you get behind schedule temporarily, because your client will understand this circumstance to be the exception to the rule, not your standard operating procedure. In my experience, you rarely come back from a poor performance on the first or even third project.

Once you achieve this level of trust with a business, other businesses take notice, and the process gets easier next time. In small markets such as ours, everyone in the industry knows one another, and most builders are doing projects in close proximity to one another; they will see your crew, your signage, your operation. Then when they talk to that other business owner, they will hear what a seamless experience it has been having your business execute a trade for them. Now you're in demand, and they'll call you; you will have GCs pursuing you instead of the other way around. Now you have the opportunity to build out a larger team, train them accordingly, and go get that next client. If you had taken that first offer of subjugation to one builder, you would still have one crew, doing what you're told and taking what you are given; you're barely self-employed at that point, much less a business owner. You are pretty much right where you started, but without the perks of being an employee.

If you do it right, the GCs and home builders in your market start to become beholden to you instead of you being beholden to one contractor.

This is a classic don't-put-all-your-eggs-in-one-basket situation. The construction industry is volatile, to say the least. You don't want to run the risk of showing up to work one day and finding out that the general contractor who has been paying your bills has gone out of business or decided to retire or maybe has a nephew who just happened to get started in your trade and is going to do all the work for the GC now.

There are so many things to go wrong with the one-to-one business-to-business relationship. I think having a minimum of three clients as soon as possible is key; even if you aren't taking on 100 percent of their work, you should be actively pursuing recurring work and building relationships with a minimum of three established general contractors. Pick up a few smaller ones along the way too; don't underestimate the value of the GC that builds two to five homes a year. These clients are usually easy to please, and it's not a big deal for you to plug in a few extra projects throughout the year, but they just might keep your men working when the bigger GCs are in a lull or waiting on subs or whatever. They're valuable, but don't rely on this type of GC. Although there are plenty of guys who run their business almost solely off contractors like this, meaning they have ten to fifteen clients instead of four, the main drawback I see is that it lends itself to the accordion effect more than working for larger businesses. A lot of these GCs will start building around the same time and finish around the same time, so if your business is concrete, let's say, you might be so busy you can barely keep up for two or three months while everyone needs foundations, then hunting down work for a couple of months, then overly busy with sidewalks and driveways, then nothing until then next foundations are ready for you, up and down all year. Same goes for every trade along the way. Another issue with the small-time builder is they are far more susceptible to market fluctuations. They likely don't have their margins dialed in as well as the larger company, and they can't afford to float out five to ten homes at a time or lose money on a project just to keep the pipeline full.

I prefer to work with larger, more established builders; they tend to be more organized, their pay schedule is usually more structured, and they have the ability to weather economic variables better than the guy who is building just a few homes. This type of GC builds roughly thirty or more homes a year, and some do commercial work too, which is great if you can handle it. They are eight-figure businesses, and they have office support, field support, laborers who can take care of things quickly for you, and competent superintendents and on-site management. They will expect more out of you, but they will do what they can to help you execute on their behalf. These are highly valuable relationships that generally provide a much steadier flow of work, with resources at their disposal. These guys don't think twice about approving a $500 change order if it needs to be done, whereas it might be a big deal for a two-home-a-year GC, who will fuck around for two days doing it himself or figuring out how to save $200. You don't have time for that shit; you have a business to run.

In conclusion, from day one, be focused on providing the highest quality of service you can to each client, but keep your eyes on the horizon. You need to be looking forward to where you want to be in a year, three years, five years. Many offers sound like a sweet deal at the time but have the potential to hamstring you from achieving what it is you set out to achieve. Make sure before you make a deal that it serves your future, not just today's needs. Keep in mind this thought too: you should be ok with moving on from business relationships. Sometimes we need a lifeboat, but once we row to shore, does it make sense to carry the boat on the rest of your journey? Just the fact that something saved you or helped you get to where you are, doesn't mean you need to keep it with you. Learn to let things that are no longer serving you go so you can move forward effectively.

CHAPTER 5

CREATING INTRAPRENEURSHIP OPPORTUNITIES

Shortly after that 2010 hailstorm I mentioned earlier, I joined up with a couple of guys I knew from high school at a company called Montana Exterior Specialists. This company, which was started by two young men, has now grown to be the primary exterior cladding contractor in the Bozeman area. They perform seven figures or more a year in business and provide excellent jobs. One of those jobs is held by my brother, Cole. He manages the flagship crew and makes a damn fine living for his family in the process.

Shawn and Eric had been in business a couple of years by that point, but it had been sporadic. Lots of traveling and gaps in work. That was the climate at the time though. The building industry was at a standstill. They had just landed a decent contract for some hail repairs when they brought me on, and shortly after, we would land a thirty-six-unit apartment building, which would help move us forward in a big way.

Shawn was the main man. Eric had started the business with Shawn but wasn't trying to grow it; he was content earning a paycheck. But Shawn wanted more. I could sense that, and that was how he got my buy-in 100 percent. I could sense we were on the same train of thought, that we were going places together.

Over the course of seven years, Shawn and I built MES into a $1.5 million company, more than tripling total sales in that time frame. Shawn ran the office end of things and worked on-site with us every day. MES was his business and his alone. Eric had failed to contribute at the level necessary to be a true partner, and a year or two after I started, we all decided it was best if he had his own separate crew. Shawn and Eric still work together to this day, and Eric contributes in a way that he is content with, as an independent contractor performing siding installation for MES.

The reason I say that we built the business, even though Shawn is the sole owner, is that was how it worked. Even though I was working for Shawn, we discussed every decision. We made decisions on hiring, on pricing, and everything else together. I invested in a few tools and things, but Shawn owned the equipment we used. Still, it was a partnership in every other way, and the way that we showed up for each other. He worked hard to make sure that we had work in front of us and the equipment to do it. In return, I made sure that I did everything in my power to get the work done on time and with brand quality. I handled meetings and customer relationships when Shawn couldn't, and we built a brand together. That brand is intact to this day because Cole, who is now in the same role as I was then, watched and learned every step of the way. He stepped into that role flawlessly and improved upon my performance considerably. This is a great example of how in the right situation, being an intrapreneur can be very effective and beneficial.

The reason for telling you about this business, and the time I spent there, is this: Shawn could've run his company differently. He could have shouted orders, taken all the credit, and paid his top-tier men less than we were worth. Lots of guys do this, but few if any of them ever make it beyond the self-employment stage of operations. They have one crew, and they work with their tool bags on every day.

Shawn invested in us, he truly valued our input, and he gave us latitude to do things our own way when it served all of us. He got us to buy in because we were directly seeing the fruits of our labor. Our pay scale was 100 percent transparent. He took a predetermined percentage for the business, and we split the rest of each job at varying rates depending on the value each of us provided.

I'm not suggesting that you must do it the same way, but whatever you decide on, follow through with transparency. Don't say one thing and then let your men catch you doing another. A high performer in an employee or independent contractor role will not tolerate being misled or lied to about their compensation or anything else for that matter. These men value the deal that you made with them; that's why they uphold their end of it consistently and are the high performers they are in life and business. They should have an opportunity to see the fruits of their labor firsthand, if possible, whether that is in the form of piece work, performance bonuses, profit share, or whatever. But under no circumstances can you say they are getting a 10 percent profit share and then give them only 5 percent. They will find out, and they will leave your ass high and dry at best, and at worst, they will become your competitors, hell bent on seeing you fail.

When someone feels valued and heard, he will go the extra mile to make things work. When you are transparent about the operations of your business with your team and about how those operations translate directly to their compensation, they develop a sense of responsibility for the business itself. Instead of a bunch of employees simply marching to your orders, you have a group of people working toward a common goal, fully applying themselves. Not everyone who works for you will take this kind of initiative, but some will, and they will become invaluable to your operation. The transparency around the compensation and the business's overall revenue, operating expenses, and margins will also ensure that your employees are not crafting their own narrative about who is making what, specifically what you are making compared with what they are making. It's a serious detriment to an operation when an employee starts guessing about how much money you make as the owner; they usually overestimate by a full decimal place or more in my experience. They will craft all kinds of scenarios and narratives around how you are getting rich and they are undercompensated. It's human nature to some extent, a primitive guard against being taken advantage of by others. But nonetheless, it usually manifests into a bad attitude, which spreads malignantly through the ranks. Some will be smart enough to just address the issue with you up front, but most will allow it to fester. So tell them. Tell them what the margins are on a project; I have learned that they are usually shocked at how little money you make on each project. Share at whatever level of comfort you wish, but ensure that they feel they are getting a piece of the pie one way or the other. It should be noted that although you should be as transparent as possible, it is also important to be precise in sharing. Maybe don't tell them the entire contract price, just the margin that will remain. Many of them will fail to think about all the expenses that the total contract price exists to cover first, before you make a dime. They will inevitably conflate total contract with profit.

Shawn was able to grow MES because he enlisted the help of like-minded men with the same level of determination he has, and he compensated them at a level at which it made sense for them to stay and help build his company. The last three years I worked with Shawn, I made over $150k a year; it's unheard of in the construction industry for a person not running their own business to make that kind of money. I was outearning every single superintendent, project manager, and office worker involved in any project we did without question, sometimes by a factor of two or more. In return for this opportunity, I made Shawn and his company look good, every day. I gave 100 percent effort. Sometimes I would even keep him on track, making sure we paid attention to the details, not just the big picture. I know for a fact that Cole does the same to this day, because he is bought in, vested in the two of them succeeding together.

If you want someone to work as hard as you do and go to battle for you to help build *your dream*, you must make it worthwhile for them. They need to be given the opportunity to build their own lives and dreams while they are helping you pursue yours. I would've never spent seven years working with MES if that hadn't been the case, and neither would my brother. Cole has worked with MES for ten years now, and he has no intention of leaving, except for retiring from the industry altogether to pursue some other dreams he has down the road. Cole is a highly capable, highly intelligent man. He could work anywhere, even start and run a business without a second thought, but he doesn't, because he is able to build his life working with Shawn and he gets to walk away from it at the end of the day if he wants. It's a win for both parties.

Right now, I have a young man who works for me who started at twenty-one years old. He has worked for me for almost four years as I'm writing this; he has proven worthy of this type of opportunity, and I have obliged him with it. He executes at a higher level than every other employee I have had past or present, and I believe he will continue to do so because I make it easy for him to help me build my business.

He made just over $100k last year as a carpenter, he drives a nice truck, he bought his wife a home, and so on and so forth. Why would he leave? He is winning at a higher level than the large majority of his peers, college educated or not, and I have held up my end of the deal by keeping him gainfully employed. Without him, I could never have taken on the workload that I did in 2021 and 2022 and would likely still be wearing my tool bags daily.

But still, other business owners will balk at the idea that I paid a carpenter six figures. They can't believe that I would "waste my money" like that when I could get someone to do it for $60k. No, I couldn't. Not like this man; he does it how I want it, in the time I want it, with the attitude I want, and he doesn't let anything stop him. He works weekends, if need be, without my direction. He solves problems, and he teaches new people. The same "business owners" who scoff at the idea are the ones who have three guys total working for them, all of whom hate them and will cut and run at the first chance if a better offer comes along.

I watched just that happen to one of these business owners. He runs a concrete business in Helena, he pays as little as he can, and he is a piss-poor leader. I have seen him sitting on a lawn chair in the middle of a foundation hole barking orders at his men as they work around him. Yeah, really, like a modern-day, fat-assed, Mountain Dew–drinking fucking slave master. One day, a competitor of his walked up to his crew when he wasn't there and offered them five dollars more an hour to come work for him, and everyone but one man just walked off that jobsite right then. It damn near put him out of business for good, and it for sure cost him considerable market share, all because he didn't treat his men like they were valuable.

Treat your employees with gratitude and patience, and give them the opportunity to build their own lives. These men are not numbers on your payroll sheet; they have wives, kids, and real dreams for the future, so you need to provide a path to those dreams, or they will find someone who will. Without employees who are truly bought in on the mission, your mission, you will never make it over the self-employment hump. You will be trapped in an endless cycle of employee turnover and frustration.

Intrapreneurship is an underappreciated skill and concept in today's business culture. There is so much "be your own boss" hype out there that it discounts the validity of being a high-performing employee. Sometimes, depending on your goals and aspirations, it's the better path, as it is for my bother. He is a driven, high-performing person, but he has no interest in running his own siding or construction company. He likes his time off; he doesn't want to be tethered to his phone and solving problems with employees on the weekend or worrying about the schedule and how it's all going to come together. Now, don't misunderstand: he does all those things—he works weekends, he manages employees, he stresses over the schedule—but he doesn't *have* to, because at the end of the day, it's not his responsibility. He can schedule a vacation and just turn his fucking phone off for a week.

He and I took a hunting trip this fall; we were out of cell coverage for five days. It took me two weeks of prep work and delegation to get ready to leave, I had to set up automatic responses, multiple alternate contacts, schedules, material deliveries, payroll—you name it. He just walked out the door and turned off his phone and didn't give it another thought. Meanwhile, even after all the prep work, I still stressed about it the whole week. All was well in the end, but as a business owner, you are never free of the responsibility of all the moving parts.

As an intrapreneur, or a high-performing employee, whichever label you prefer, you get many of the perks of owning your own business without many of the drawbacks. You can set boundaries with your time, and as long as you perform and execute, they will be respected. You reap the benefits of a company that you are helping to grow, without making any financial investments yourself. You will invest your time and energy, but those are low-risk investments, especially when a guaranteed paycheck is attached to them. Although there are many positive aspects to this path, there are some drawbacks. The primary issue with intrapreneurship is that at some point there is a ceiling to your earning potential. You may earn a considerable living, well into six figures in some cases. But at the end of the day, no one is going to pay you $500k a year to work inside their construction company because someone who can do the job at or above the required level will do it for $100k, and the highest-performing, most qualified men with a battery of skills that outclass your own will do it for $250k.

So when considering this path, make sure that the amount of money you need to achieve the goals and dreams you have fits within what is a realistic salary in whatever company you choose. On the other side of the coin, as a business owner, be realistic about the type of person you want in those higher-up positions and what kind of money they need to make to be satisfied. These are high achievers, and they will walk and find a better opportunity or outright become your competition if you aren't taking care of them in a meaningful way.

CHAPTER 6

CREATING A BRAND AND A CONSISTENT CUSTOMER EXPERIENCE

At SCE Inc., it has been and continues to be my goal to completely monopolize the exteriors market in the Helena area. I want to put every motherfucker out there out of business and have a job waiting for them at my company. I don't have any ill will or animosity to the other tradesmen out there; I just want to be the best. I want to be able to say unabashedly that SCE Inc. Is the only exterior cladding company in Helena worth hiring, or even that there is to hire. I know that sounds extreme, but it must be the goal, or you won't ever get even halfway there. We are already the industry leader, and we are chewing up more market share every day. Many exterior siding and roofing contractors already look to us to help fill their pipeline with work, which we gladly do if they are reputable and trustworthy, for a percentage of each job, with noncompetition agreements in place, of course. It's a positive interaction for both businesses, but I believe it goes to show the amount of the market for our services that we are controlling.

The main component of this success has been our consistent on-brand performance. When SCE Inc. shows up to a project, everyone there, from the general contractor to the guy taping drywall inside, knows what is about to happen. My crew is about to blow the fucking doors off this project. They will put the siding on that house in three days, not twelve like the guy next door, do a better job than anyone else in town, and leave the jobsite cleaner than when they showed up. We have a reputation, a brand, whatever you want to call it; people know what to expect when our crews roll up. This is critical to the growth and maintenance of a company, and it must remain in place as you scale. This is a basic and well-known principle in business, but it can be extremely difficult to achieve in the construction industry.

The construction industry is full of unpredictability, most of which is created by the type of people who are employed within it. Sadly, many of the stereotypes are spot-on; some in construction are crackhead, trailer-trash shit bags who pull up in a car with an off-color door, turn on some death metal, and light a cigarette before they get started. These guys are going nowhere in life by their own design, so that's how they work, and those are the kinds of results they produce, for you as well as themselves. But since there is a critical shortage of men to work in these industries, they get hired and set the stage for the construction industry to be plagued with delayed schedules and workmanship issues. So when you can create stability in this chaotic industry by producing consistent results, you become indispensable. Contractors will pay a significant premium for your services if they know for a fact that they can count on you to follow through and produce the results they are accustomed to seeing out of your company.

There are several key factors that contribute to creating a brand in the construction industries, or any blue-collar industry for that matter. We often don't have the luxury of gatekeepers white collar professionals enjoy, such as front-desk girls or call centers, directing people to the right person to talk to in any given situation.

Hiring, retaining, and properly placing quality employees is of the utmost importance. "Duh," you say, but it's a little more complex than that in this space. Sometimes you'll have a guy who is a rock star at his trade but is terrible at talking to customers or just people in general; maybe he has a temper or is a "no filter" kind of guy. That guy is a liability. He will flip out on your best client in a moment of frustration, or he'll neglect to turn the offensive music off or watch his language when the homeowner's family is doing a walk through. You say, "Well, fire his ass!" Boom, problem solved. No?

Here is where it gets complicated. You still absolutely, undoubtedly need that guy. If you fired guys like this every time they did something like that in this industry, you would work by yourself, forever. It's the nature of the beast, but you must learn to tame it. This kind of employee needs to have someone they answer to on the jobsite. It may not even be someone who knows more than they do about the trade, but someone who can communicate effectively and knows when to stop talking or to call you. You must designate who is allowed to talk to clients and homeowners and who isn't. Some of these guys have no filter and can't be trusted to make good decisions about communicating with the people who cut your checks and keep the work coming. Some guys can be trained and taught how to do it; others can't or won't. You need to be able to recognize which ones you are dealing with.

Keep in mind some of these guys have had wild lives; they grew up in trailers with white-trash dads who had no filter and worked in the construction industry, or didn't work at all, so they always got away with it, and then they spent every nonworking hour in some dive bar where the conversation was anything but tasteful. They can get to thinking some pretty off-color shit is just normal conversation, so when you tell them to be polite and respectful, they might have every intent of doing so but legitimately just don't know how or what you mean when you say that. They are nice guys and mean no harm, but they think using the words "cunt" or "motherfucker" in a conversation falls in the polite category because they were nice about it or at least they didn't call anyone a cunt; they just said it—a "cunt hair" is a commonly used unit of measurement, but you already know that if you are reading this. I have heard those exact words spoken to a female architect before: "This little spot is a real motherfucker, but if we take a cunt hair off this, we can make it work." That guy was just explaining something in his own words. The woman he was talking to was flabbergasted, looking at him with horror. After all, she had left an office not ten minutes ago where that kind of talk would result in a cleaned-out desk and a pending lawsuit, and he didn't even notice. Thankfully he wasn't getting his paycheck from me, but it could've just as easily been one of my guys if I didn't have a plan for that kind of thing. Don't let that guy talk to your clients—or anyone really.

I had one of my first employees pull something like this once, and that's how I know. This guy's name was Derek. He was a wild card, and he was a good hand and reliable, but his interpersonal skills were unpredictable. He would often say things that made no sense, terribly off color, and sometimes have full-blown conversations with himself at full volume. In hindsight, the guy was clearly displaying some mental health issues, but I didn't have much choice but to work around them. One day we were working on a project for a contractor we no longer do business with but who at the time was our meal ticket; they were building more than half of our total volume. The owner of this company was a stuck-up, self-important ass, and everyone knew it, but his checks cleared.

The owner of this $20 million-a-year company walked onto our jobsite to check on a couple of things and said something to Derek. I was probably forty yards away and heading over there to talk to him, afraid of what Derek might say, when I heard Derek say, "Why don't you make yourself useful and clean this shit up?" as he tried to hand him a trash can.

I about fucking died. My inner child laughed, but my entrepreneur side was mortified. How could you think that was a good thing to say to anyone? Much less that guy? I mean holy fuck, man, there wasn't anything worse you could have said to a guy like that.

I kind of barked at Derek and said something to the effect of "What the hell, man? That's the owner of X company; *you* clean this shit up!" With a nervous laugh I tried to brush it off with the owner, and to his credit, he didn't make a big deal about it. It amounted to nothing, as it was not his first encounter with a wild-card construction worker either, but it taught me a valuable lesson.

Those boundaries need to be set, day one: Who is allowed to talk to our clients? Who is allowed to talk schedule? Talk money? Other than hello and how are you, the rest of your team needs to stay out of it. There should be one point of contact per crew, at least until they have been with you long enough to learn your culture and how to communicate appropriately with clients and customers.

Clear and calm communication should be something you strive for on the first day of the first project and every day thereafter. So many owner operators, guys who know how to execute their trade but not necessarily how to execute on a business, are worthless at communicating. They say one thing and do another, make unrealistic schedules they have no intention of or means of honoring, fly off the handle about insignificant things, and so on and so forth. This creates the opposite of a consistent experience. Imagine trying to schedule ten different trades on a job during any given stage of a project, not knowing if one or more of them will be there when they say they will be. It's a compounding disaster that costs every involved party precious time and money.

Now flip that scenario on its head. Everyone else is showing up late, taking too long, not doing it to specifications, and you ride in on a white stallion, on time, and execute your contractual duties with efficiency and professionalism *every fucking time*. If you do that, why on earth would they even consider hiring anyone else for your scope of work? It won't be long before they don't even bother getting competing estimates, because they know for a fact they can count on you to perform. It's not worth a few thousand dollars, even on a small project such as a spec house, to gamble on whether the siding, roofing, plumbing, HVAC, or whatever will get done on time or to a warranty specification.

As a quick side note to the concept above, once that level of execution has been established with a client, it opens up opportunity for you to expand into other scopes of work for the same contactor if you are so inclined, as long as you are certain you can execute at the same level in all of them—you cannot be a great HVAC contractor, take on the plumbing, do a marginal job, and expect it not to affect the relationship for both trades. You are selling yourself and your ability to perform, period.

It's also not worth it for the manager of that project to gamble on the *personality* that shows up with a different subcontractor. Some people never learn how to communicate or deal with conflict in a professional manner. A framing contractor who used to work for one of my best clients lost a forty- to fifty-home-a-year contract because he had a temper and an abrasive, obstructionist attitude. He would make problems appear out of thin air and throw a fit over the smallest inconveniences. He provided a consistent customer experience all right: consistent turmoil and animosity. Although he was arguably one of the most skilled framers in the area, he lost his only contract because of his attitude and poor communication skills. He traded $800k a year in sales—his total sales, mind you—for the opportunity to be a cocksucker. He also made another blunder: he was operating on a one-to-one business-to-business ratio, like we talked about earlier in the book. His personality and personal issues cost him his single customer and effectively bounced him back to the starting line. I'm no Warren Buffet, but that's just plain bad business.

Now, as you likely already know, the construction industry is not like your average office environment. It's nothing out of the ordinary to have a shouting match between people on the jobsite, or sometimes even a physical altercation. Nobody calls HR; we just move through it and find a way forward most of the time. But nobody likes it. Everyone would prefer a calm, professional work environment with clear and concise communication and firm boundaries about what they will and won't do and tolerate within their scope of work and the execution of their job duties.

It's a tough line to walk, because the construction industry is so rough around the edges, it's easy to get sloppy with your professionalism. You will get away with so much bullshit because you are dealing with thick-skinned, alpha-type people day in and day out. But at the end of the day, you are not trying to get away with bad behavior and get a few projects. You are building a business that needs to have a steady flow of work from the best contractors, a business whose reputation precedes it in the best way possible. You can't afford to have one subcontractor, or worse yet a general contractor, talking shit about you. Your execution should be so consistent that the only thing that can be said about you is the truth about your incredible performance. Companies that are looking to hire subcontractors should only need to hear your name to know they are going to hire you.

On the flipside, you must have a backbone. But it must be predictable. You will run into other trades and new GCs who want to push the envelope with you, and you must stand your ground, or they will walk all over you. Remember you are dealing with assertive, sometimes aggressive individuals, some of whom are just looking to have a problem.

A common problem for any tradesman is the other guy's stuff is in your way—a truck, a lift, a pallet whatever. It's a common source of animosity for no reason. Obviously if you ask nicely, there isn't a problem 95 percent of the time. On occasion, it becomes an issue. If someone needs you to move something, if it's not a big deal for you, move the goddamn thing; don't be the asshole who acts like his work is more important than the next guy's. Sometimes you can't accommodate a request, or it will be considerably harder for you to move than for them to work around you. Just explain that situation, end the conversation, and move on. Don't be a dick, and don't yell; just apologize for the inconvenience and move on. It won't take long until you develop a reputation as a reasonable guy who does what he can to be accommodating, but if he can't, he won't. People will find a way to work around you. Do this simple thing, and you will avoid a hundred shouting matches in your career. It applies to almost any situation where there is some form of disagreement. Be accommodating to a point, but stand your ground on the things that actually matter to you or affect your bottom line.

Finally, your work itself must be consistent. You must be able to replicate the same product, over and over, with few alterations. In the siding industry, it's pretty straightforward. The siding must be installed to warranty specifications and look presentable. In addition, it must be done the way each client likes as far as the details go. In other trades it may be a little less obvious, but I would work toward having a standard installation for everything. Train your men how you want it done, and uphold the standard on every job without exception. Never let your men see you say "good enough" or "that will fly" unless it is truly good enough, meeting the standard you have set.

If your client cannot tell the difference between each job you do for them, you are doing it right. Imagine a great restaurant that has the best steaks, and that's why you go there: you get a delicious ribeye cooked properly, and you enjoy your meal. But next week, the same place serves you an overcooked round steak for the same price. My guess is you won't be visiting that restaurant anymore. Same goes for a tradesman and any other type of service industry. It all comes down to creating a consistent, predictable, and positive customer experience with every crew on every job.

CHAPTER 7

SELLING YOUR SERVICES AT A PREMIUM VERSUS THE COMPETITION

This is an interesting one in the blue-collar space: How do I get more for the same project than the next guy?

Become a value-added trade partner. Period. End of chapter. It could be summed up that quickly, but what does that entail?

Becoming a value-added trade partner is just like it sounds. You add value over and above the competition. This can be done any number of ways, but the key is that you give something more than the next guy. It doesn't have to cost you anything, it doesn't have to be a big deal, but you need to create the perception that you are worth more money for the same project than the next guy, then be able to articulate how that is the case. You already know why you are better; now your customer or client needs to be educated.

Some of the ways to prove this are obvious to most of us—the first one being to do a better job. Do a higher standard of work, whatever that means in your field. For some trades it's easy to tell and requires little to no explanation to the client, such as in siding: it's mostly visual, so if your siding project looks better than the next guy's, it likely is better, with few exceptions. There are some things that will require explanation so that your client understands why and how you are doing a better job. Careful with this though; you want to avoid sounding like a blowhard who is trying to *sell the idea* that you are the best. Nobody likes that salesmanship bullshit, and they will see right through it. This is often a sign that a tradesman doesn't know what he is doing, is desperate for work, or both.

Take the time to educate your client on your process, how it differs from the competition's, and how it produces the desired results for the client. Most general contractors don't care about the intricacies of each individual trade or exactly how you do your job; they just want it done right, which is why they hired you. Don't get lost in the weeds explaining every little thing to them. Hit the high points, be prepared for any questions, and be well read on the products you are using, so much so that you can recite the warranty specifications and requirements accurately. This alone will give your client confidence that you know what you are doing and that they have entrusted their project to the right subcontractor. You are supposed to be a professional, so make sure you have a professional level of knowledge.

This concept is not only about being the best electrician, framer, or plumber. It's as much about you and what else you bring to the table as it is about who does the best job, because for the most part you can only be incrementally better than the other businesses in your trade at the actual trade, the actual install or fabrication aspect, because any work needs to meet industry standards and pass inspections. You can improve here and there, but most of those incremental improvements are lost on the customer and go unnoticed. What you can improve drastically on is your service. You can blow your competition out of the water on schedule, communication, and accountability. If you can master these three things, you become hugely valuable to your customers and clients.

Finally, don't get hung up on getting paid for every little change order or inconvenience you encounter; that shit is annoying. Subcontractors have a reputation for being prima donnas, a reputation for making mountains out of molehills. When you call a GC or superintendent four times a day, telling him every little issue on the jobsite, you become the problem, not the solution. So if something is going to take ten or fifteen minutes to fix—hell, even an hour sometimes—just do it if you are capable. Or if it's outside your wheelhouse completely, call the guy whose trade it is first, not the GC. The fewer times you must talk to your GC during the course of a project, the better for both of you.

This was a short chapter because it's a simple concept. No math, no metrics, just exceptional service paired with work to the industry standard or better.

CHAPTER 8

THE THREE PILLARS OF A CONSTRUCTION BUSINESS

There are three critically important, indispensable pillars that will make or break your business. These simple concepts are the foundation on which everything else rests and can either support your business or let it crumble. Any time you are evaluating your business plan or performance, you should audit these areas first; if you are having issues, it's likely related to one of these areas.

SCHEDULING

Schedule is so important in construction. That's why it's mentioned over and over in this book. If you can keep a coherent schedule, you are way ahead of the game. It's much harder than it sounds, so don't take it for granted. One strategy I use to ensure my scheduling is as accurate as possible is tracking every project my teams do. I look at how big it is and how much of each material is present, I identify the possible challenges they will face due to site conditions, and then I make a projection of how long it will take. Once I have my projection, I inform the team what I expect and discuss it with them to see whether they agree or have some other input. Over the course of hundreds of projects, my predictions have become increasingly accurate, and yours will too. But you can get a handle on this in just a handful of projects for each team; you will quickly learn who is best at what, who is fastest, and who is most detail oriented, so you can allocate manpower to the project that most suits each team. Once you implement this simple system, your scheduling will become far more accurate. You will still have to deal with weather delays and delays from other trades, but those are out of your control. Control what you can.

Another important aspect of scheduling is learning to be flexible. A schedule is a living, malleable thing. If you try to apply rigidity to it, it breaks and becomes useless. The fact that project 1 was scheduled ahead of projects 2 and 3 doesn't mean that's the order you are going to be doing them in. Delays, cancelations, and other issues all happen frequently. Be prepared to switch things around and make new plans. When doing so, communicate with your clients about it. Explain why, how long until you're back, and how they can avoid this in the future. Most GCs are understanding about this constant shuffle, to a point. It becomes your job to do triage on who is going to be most tolerant of delay and who is not. But be careful of always making the same client wait; just the fact that they are cooperative and patient doesn't mean they will always tolerate being last in line. You may show up to your next project for them one day and find your competitor in your place. Try to be judicious with your scheduling. If someone is ready for you when they said they would be, they should get top priority. If they are not ready, simply move to the next client in line.

An important aspect to this is building out your team in such a way that each crew, each team member is capable of doing the full range of work you may encounter. Obviously, some crews will be better at one type of job or another, but everyone should be able to do the range of work your company performs. This ensures that in a scheduling pinch, you can allocate any crew that has time or better fits the schedule. Being stuck waiting on your A team is not ideal, so all your teams should be the A team as much as possible given the differences of humans and their abilities and skill sets. In short, don't stack all your talent on one crew and all the misfits on the other; put a tiered set of workers on each crew when possible. One leadership position, one skilled position, and one labor position per crew is ideal in my opinion.

Additionally, although it's inevitable sometimes, avoid leaving a job unfinished to go start another one if you can help it. I see this all the time—guys bouncing back and forth between two or three jobs at a time. Each time they relocate, they lose production and efficiency, ultimately costing them time and putting them further behind. You will be stuck on those three projects for far longer than they would have taken if you did them one at a time, and by the time you finally finish, you may find that your other clients have moved on and replaced you. It might be only temporary, but that is a problem you dare not invite. If instead you make a habit of doing every project start to finish and your clients know this, they will be more patient, knowing that when you land on their project, the end is in sight and it will be done before you leave. I make that promise every time I start with a new contractor, and we hold to it as long as they can do their job and keep the work in front of us while we are there.

COMMUNICATION

Communication is key to any relationship. Communication with your customers and clients is no different. You must always keep a clear channel of communication open with them. Make sure you know what projects they have coming up and what their expectations of you are regarding those projects. Don't assume anything. Beyond that, once you land on a project, make sure you clearly communicate the schedule, any possible issues you see, and any change orders that will be required. Don't just send a bill that's $500 more than the estimate without an explanation or a heads-up. When people get upset, it almost always boils down to a lack of communication or miscommunication. Your client may not be excited to hear that you must do $500 worth of unanticipated extras to complete your job properly, but they will understand, and they won't be surprised when they get the bill. On the other hand, if you just do it, don't communicate with anyone about it, and send the bill, they are going to be upset because they weren't part of the process. You quickly go from looking like the guy who solved a problem for them to looking like the problem.

The same goes for not showing up to a project on time. If you tell them Tuesday and don't show until Friday, there is going to be an issue. On the other hand, if you elaborate on the situation a little ahead of time and explain that you hope to be on-site by Tuesday, but that is reliant on a number of factors, so it could be as late as Friday, nobody is upset; they knew there was a range of dates and that you would keep them in the loop as things moved along. Give yourself the time you need to ensure that you can arrive on time for your clients. I will never understand the guy who tells you Monday when you and he both know damn well it won't be until Wednesday, but it's an all-too-common occurrence in this industry.

ACCOUNTABILITY

Scheduling and communication are great, but if you lack accountability to them, they are worthless. Just hot air out of your mouth with no actions attached. I reiterate this to my team almost on a daily basis.

You must be accountable to the things you say. When you make a schedule, hold yourself and your team accountable to it. If you fail, be accountable and take responsibility for the role you and your team played in that failure. When you communicate with your clients, be sure you intend to and have the capacity to follow through with the promises you are making. If you say you can and will do something, you damn well better follow through.

There is no faster way to make your business a memory than failure to hold yourself and your team accountable to the promises that were made. At the end of the day, all you have to sell as a tradesman is your word, your word that you will do what you said you would do when you said you would do it. That's your whole product; the actual work is just the byproduct of what you said you would do and that people took your word for it. If they stop believing you, you stop getting the work. Maintain accountability at all costs: work the weekends to make up a schedule, bring in more manpower if needed—do whatever it takes to ensure that your client knows you are holding yourself accountable to the promises you made to them. If you do this, in earnest, they will be more likely to forgive you for dropping the ball on occasion, which is inevitable.

CHAPTER 9

SETTING AND MAINTAINING A PRICE POINT

This, like many other things, is not as cut-and-dried in the construction industry as it is elsewhere. There is often much secrecy surrounding pricing for subcontract work. Some don't want to share because they are worried that they will get outdone on price. Others are strangely worried about others getting as much or more than they are, like somehow they are the only ones who deserve to make X amount on a certain trade. General contractors hold this information close to the vest as well; they don't want their competitors to get the same deal they are getting, every dollar of margin counts, and the better your margins are compared with your competition, the more likely you are to grow as a business.

Whatever the reason, it makes setting a price point difficult. This is why you see wild fluctuations in the pricing across certain trades. In our market right now, I know of a company that charges $4.50 a square foot for frame construction, and I know another that is charging $12.50. That is a massive difference—an almost 300 percent uprate. Guess what: they are both booked solid months at a time. Let's use this as an example to illustrate the nuance of setting a price.

Contractor A, the $4.50 guy, is running on a bare-bones margin. He can barely pay his men, his tools are in disrepair, and he is waiting on every check, sweating the bills. His low-ball pricing will keep him making wages forever; there is no profit to be had. Nobody is going to tell him his pricing is so low, because it benefits everyone, including his competitors. How, you ask? Obviously, the GCs are making more money off him, plain and simple. But his competitors in the frame construction business benefit because he is always going to be stuck down there, as a wage-earning self-employed contractor. He can't invest in new equipment or more skilled workers. He is not really a threat in the grand scheme of things.

In setting such low rates, he has also created a perception of inexperience and vulnerability around his company that is unattractive to larger clients. He may land some projects from them, but he will never become their go-to guy because they know he could close shop any day. He might get burned out and quit, or his guys will quit to find better-paying jobs or because he couldn't cover payroll on time. Clients fear he will be unable to cover expenses that arise from unexpected circumstances, perhaps a costly mistake on his part that he can't afford to fix, leaving them holding the bill. All in all, this guy is in a bad spot. He may figure it out someday, but then he has the mountain to climb of raising his prices drastically and keeping his clients at the same time.

Contractor B, the $12.50 guy, in my opinion, fits into one of two categories. He is either content with sporadic work that pays well and does a damn fine job so he can justify charging a premium, in which case he isn't an issue for you, as he picks off one or two jobs here and there, usually from small time operations, or when the big operations get so busy even you can't keep up. He is more of an asset to you than anything. You know you can confidently recommend him to clients you don't want to service or can't service, and he will do a good job but not keep you from getting work in the future because of his inflated pricing.

Or in the second category, he has tried to scale his business too quickly and flashily. This guy isn't bad at business—far better than the $4.50 guy—but is still going to run into issues. He started to do well and decided to go for it. He bought all new equipment and hired twenty guys and scattered them across four projects. His efficiency fell off a cliff, and he quickly realized his profit model was broken, but instead of looking inward, he decided it must be that he wasn't getting paid enough. He raised prices to accommodate for lack of efficiency and production. Thus is born a house of cards. Soon his clients will grow tired of this new elevated pricing, coupled with reduced performance, and look elsewhere. His business will contract back to a smaller size and potentially fail altogether. There is a chance, however, that if he manages to provide exceptional service and accountability to his clients, he will remain in business, making considerable profit and become a formidable competitor for your market. In that event, you can learn from him; he is clearly onto something. After all, there must be a reason that he was able to charge a premium for his services and maintain his clientele. We talked about it in a different chapter; he is clearly a value-add trade partner.

Now, what should you do to avoid these pitfalls? First and foremost, do as much research as possible on the pricing for your trade in your area. Don't rely on national or even regional data from the internet; it's never accurate enough, as prices fluctuate considerably from market to market, even when they are geographically close together. Socioeconomic factors play a huge role. Nicer towns cost more to live in and pay tends to be higher, but so is the cost of living. You must take your area's socioeconomic structure into account when trying to establish a baseline for pricing.

I mean you need to do on-the-ground research. Get creative; do whatever you have to do, within the bounds of legality and morality, to find out what people are charging for your trade. Sometimes it will take a little digging, but other times they will happily share. Once you have a price range, you want to start slightly above center. Using our example, $8.50 a foot is the middle. So you charge $9.00. Go out and bid work at $9.00 and see what you get. You shouldn't get every project. You want one out of four guys to say your price is too high. If everyone accepts right away, you have a strong indication your price is too low. If you get shot down because of pricing 50 percent of the time, you are too high. Find that market tolerance and figure out a way to make your business work, to make your profit model work at that rate and with enough cushion that you could absorb a minimum 10 percent reduction in price. This will help insulate you from fluctuating housing market conditions and give you time to react, and it will help in tough times when work is tougher to come by.

Once you have established a price point, you must honor it. When I send an estimate, that thing is gospel for one year. Granted, we only sell our labor, no materials. Barring any changes by the customer, I will honor that rate for one year. At the first of every year, I evaluate the pricing, market conditions, and our profit model based on last year's performance and decide where our prices need to go for quoting new projects. Naturally, pricing should trend upward for inflation, but sometimes the market won't support it. Prices should be lowered only if the market is in a serious downturn and you are really hurting for work, as a matter of survival, but that's a dangerous road. You are telling your clients that you don't value your work as much as you did a month ago. Some may even translate that to mean they have been paying you too much and you have been ripping them off.

I tend to look at 5 percent increases in a year, if *necessary*, as reasonable. Beyond that, GCs are going to raise eyebrows unless there is a good, communicable reason for raising prices by more. In 2021, I raised pricing 7.5 percent because inflation was at or around that rate. It wasn't a big deal; all my clients understood. But like I have said a dozen times in this book already, clear communication is critical.

You can't just spring that on your clients without explanation. Go to their office and explain the situation. Any time you raise pricing, tell them what to expect and why you are doing it. They will understand. If they don't, so be it, because you *need* to get 5 percent or 10 percent more, right? You must stick to your guns with this. If you back down when they object to the pricing, you will be stuck at the same rate forever. Have some backbone and make sure the decision to increase price was made from necessity, not out of greed. Be ready to lose a client over it, although if you approach it like I just explained, it is unlikely to happen. If you can't get paid what you need from a customer, continuing to work with them is a detriment to your business.

Be consistent with your pricing too; don't let yourself get greedy when you just had an expensive month or things aren't going your way. It's all too common to hear someone talking about how they got way more for this or that project, for reasons that don't make any sense, other than they got greedy the day they did the bid work. Find your rate, establish your margins, and maintain a consistent price point for each project—and for each type of work, for that matter.

STRUCTURE OF PRICING

There are a couple of ways to structure pricing. One is to simply charge the same amount for every client. This is an effective strategy and keeps things simple. In many ways, it legitimizes the pricing you have chosen. The price is the price, period. I know of several contractors that run this system with great results.

On the other hand, you can have a graduated pricing structure. This is what I personally do. It's slightly more complex to manage, but I strongly believe it improves my bottom line. Let me explain. I try to tailor my pricing to each contractor. It takes time, and you must do a couple of projects with them to understand where you need to be on price point, so I always try to go in at my midlevel pricing with new clients; this is one part giving them the benefit of the doubt and one part covering your ass.

Some GCs make it easy. They are always ready and organized, use readily available materials, and have a laborer who can do punch-list items, so you don't have to make two or three trips to the same job to screw in a lightbulb or install the door that was back ordered. They also give you 100 percent of their projects. These clients should get the lowest rate on the scale. They make it easy; their efficiency creates wider margins for you. Therefore, you can afford to offer a better price point. Make sure they know it too. They will love to hear they are getting a better deal than the next guy.

Larger-volume clients will also often expect lower pricing in exchange for the considerable volume of work they provide you. It's a very simple economic principle: you buy more, you pay less. Costco exists solely on this premise. Be certain that before you commit to pricing you have your margin dialed in so you are still profitable performing their work. Many a tradesman has hamstrung himself in this very way—ask me how I know.

Next you have another set of clients. They are still loyal and profitable clients, but things are not as streamlined. They may be doing more custom projects with special-order materials, they short you on material, or the schedule is a mess, and you must make multiple trips to the project almost every time. In order to maintain your margin with this type of client, they will need to pay a premium. Don't price gouge, because they will just find someone else, but bump your rate by 5–10 percent to cover some of the delays and lack of efficiency. Unlike the other client, you don't need to share that they are paying more than everyone else. If they press you on it, or discover that they are, just be honest and offer solutions to get them to that base level pricing. They will likely understand; they know as well as you do that things are not running smoothly.

Third is the one-off client; they get the highest price point. Again, you aren't trying to gouge and get a ridiculous uprate, but you need to consider the fact that you will have to go through more admin work per dollar with this client than any other. On the jobsite, your team will have to get up to speed with a new client and their preferences and work out the kinks all for one or two jobs. That all costs money. I tack on 15 percent to my base rate for this type of client until we start getting more of or all their work.

As an exception to this, if you have a client who may be giving you only one or two projects right now but has the potential to dole out significantly more work in the near future, consider giving that client the midrange price point, as you don't want to exclude yourself from future consideration for contracts because the client thinks your work is too expensive.

There is so much nuance in the pricing structure of a construction business that entire books could be and have been written on it alone. Whatever you do, however you structure it, make sure you are checking in on it frequently. Run the numbers as you go to make sure you are making the margin you need. Keep your finger on the pulse of the market so you don't overshoot or get left behind. If you are clear and truthful about your pricing and have data to back it up, most contractors will be understanding about some increase in pricing over time, and you should be able to maintain a consistent margin. If the market is skyrocketing like it did in '20 and '21, edge your pricing up, but don't go crazy. And the same applies to a market contraction. If things crash, hold your pricing; if you feel like you must, edge downward to secure work, but never below your last pricing increase. Keep in mind what you need as a margin; do not chase it down the rabbit hole. Doing that devalues your work and everyone else's work for years to come.

CHAPTER 10

MANAGING BURNOUT

What do you do when you just can't anymore? The next step is critical and may determine the trajectory of your entire business and career. Below is a detailed account of what can happen when your fail to identify and properly manage burnout.

In the fall of 2017, I had been in the industry for a full decade, I was twenty-eight years old, I had a baby on the way, and my wife, Sarah, was planning on being a stay-at-home mom. I had been working with MES for almost seven years, and I unilaterally decided to go my own way. I was burned out and felt that with the arrangement we had, I was topped out. I was exhausted; we worked four days a week for twelve hours a day or more. We worked hard too, always hustling, with no breaks. Whether it was ten degrees or a hundred degrees, I was covered in concrete siding dust, bandaged fingers, and stitches, and I had overuse injuries on half the joints in my body. I remember so vividly that putting my tool bags on every morning felt like a herculean task; it took every ounce of discipline I possessed just to get that far in the day. I mentally couldn't fucking do it anymore.

We parted ways amicably after we finished a handful of projects. Now this part is important: I didn't just walk away; I had made a plan with the guys at MES and honored it, so the split was clean. I simply didn't see a better future while in that position. We had come a long way in those seven years, from barely scraping together the work we needed in 2010 to a near multimillion-dollar business. But I felt we were at a standstill. We all were making six-figure incomes, owned homes, drove new trucks, and had boats and campers; we had the lives that most construction workers dream of, but I felt I couldn't keep pounding nails every day forever to maintain that lifestyle. I wanted something different, something more.

I had been making moves in that direction for quite a while. I had been a real estate agent for several years at this point, doing a considerable amount of business on the side of the daily construction grind. Most of the time, I was handling three or four deals at a time, and sometimes up to ten; that's a full-time job in and of itself. I was answering real estate questions and scheduling showings, standing thirty feet off the ground on a scaffolding plank with my tool bags on, preparing and sending documents on my laptop at lunch. I would keep a change of clothes in my car so that I could schedule meetings and showings at lunchtime or directly after work. In hindsight, this obviously contributed to the burnout. I was doing too much to maintain for a long period of time; I juggled these two professions for four years, doing both at a high level. I was on the best siding crew in the county and would occasionally land on the top-producing agent list from month to month.

I also took a leap in 2016 and started building spec houses. The real estate market was heating up, and I had some serious FOMO. I felt like I was missing an opportunity. I did the spec thing a little differently from most tradesmen. Instead of trying to do much of the work myself, I committed to doing it 100 percent "briefcase"; I would hire out every trade, even siding. This would make it a fully separate venture that had to have its own legs. The margins at the time weren't great historically. On the first one in Belgrade, Montana, I made just over $30k, slightly under 10 percent. But to me at that time, that was significant. It helped give me the courage to take the steps I thought would lead me away from my indenture to construction labor.

So the stage was set: I had worked my ass off for ten years pounding nails, four of which I was also a successful Realtor, and the last six months I was also a home builder in tandem. In hindsight it was no wonder I was tired and strung out. Nonetheless, I kept moving.

Once I gave MES notice I would be leaving, I went to work making sure I could navigate the transition financially. I had already started the process of my second spec home, this time in Livingston, Montana, thirty minutes from home. Then I secured some siding jobs to pay the bills while I got things moving. The first siding project I started the week after I gave notice, but I was still working forty-five-plus hours with the guys. I would work all day, then head to Belgrade at 6 p.m. and work until dark or beyond, to 10 or 11 p.m. I pulled fifteen-hour days for two weeks to get that project done on time for my new client. I knew it was temporary. I just willed myself through it, convinced I would feel better once I wasn't working with MES anymore and had my autonomy completely.

Over the next couple of months, the lesson I should've learned on that first solo project was learned the hard way; apparently that's my default method of learning in life. The lesson was that I was burned out on the trade completely, and work in general, because of my failure to address the issue up front.

I struggled to produce the results I was accustomed to seeing from myself. I hired my cousin Blake to come work with me, promising him work through December, when he would leave to go teach skiing in Colorado. We worked for a few months. I struggled to make work, but I was tired, so fucking tired. Then at the end of November I just fucking quit; for the first time in my life I just capitulated.

I still get a lump in my throat when I think about it, for so many reasons. I left Blake hanging a month short of work that he had planned on, and I bailed on the contractor whose siding we were doing with almost no notice. It wasn't a good look, but I didn't think I could do it for even one more day; I was that sick of strapping on my tool bags.

Bad as that all is, and out of integrity with the values and principles I have held all my life, the part that makes me sick to this day is that my son was less than a month old, and I just quit on the primary source of income for my family. I didn't see it then, but looking back, it's painfully obvious how weak and foolish I was at that moment. It goes to show how bad burnout can get.

This decision, made from a place of emotion, of desperation for a change, would lead to the most stressful twelve months of my life, to fully self-inflicted financial stress and suffering. It would create so much anxiety in my and my family's life that it gave me a permanent heart arrhythmia; seriously, that fucker doesn't work right to this day.

I spent the beginning of 2018 wrapping up the spec house in Livingston. I purchased a lot in Manhattan and began one there too; that home would be larger and higher end than the others. I also took on a semicustom home for an older lady next door to the spec in Livingston. I had some irons in the fire and was feeling confident in the trajectory of the future. I might have been successful with all this had I just focused, but I was still trying to solve an internal problem with external solutions. Instead of focusing on the tasks at hand and trying to maximize the opportunity in front of me, I was looking for a new place to live, because I was still displeased with my life and struggling to find the motivation to execute at a high level. It became a game of whack-a-mole trying to tamp down one problem at a time, but in reality there was only one problem: I ran away from my problem instead of working to manage it appropriately.

So instead of looking inward and analyzing the situation, I decided it must be *where I live* that is the issue. So I searched MLS and Zillow daily looking for the property that would finally bring me calm, peace, and motivation.

I located a property that fit the bill in Helena. It was the type of place I had always wanted to live and raise my kids. It has a decent little house and barn, twenty-four acres that borders a few thousand acres of BLM land; I can go hiking and hunting right out my back door. My wife, Sarah, and I decided to make the move, and we purchased our home. It's still our home, and we love it here and have no plans to leave. I would do it again without a doubt, but at the time in 2018, this decision caused a considerable amount of extra stress. We closed on our home in May, and we packed our lives into boxes and our six-month-old in his car seat and moved to Helena.

At this point, I was committed to building a spec house in Manhattan, a custom home in Livingston, and a real estate business to get off the ground in Helena. What could go wrong? Everything, as it turned out.

Both building projects moved along fine. We wrapped up on the Manhattan house in August and had an offer in place to close in September. We would've done well on this offer, making $60k on the property, so naturally, it fell through. That house spent the next six months on the market, slowly draining my bank account one interest payment at a time.

The custom home project was a huge pain in the ass; it was three hours from home, and the client was a nightmare. I lay awake every night stressing about that project, begging for it to be over. I thought about quitting a dozen times, but I powered through.

All that aside, the real estate business was my primary focus once we made the move to Helena. I had been working with a broker in Bozeman for several years. His company was Boost Realty. He agreed to allow me to open a separate office under the name.

I went to work trying to get Boost Realty established in Helena. Ryan Olsen, my broker, was more than generous in helping me get going. He didn't take a dime of the commissions I made in Helena. I started marketing immediately after we an accepted offer on our home, so by the time we landed there, I had been sending out mailers and showing my face around town for several months. I blanketed the area with Every Door Direct Mail, thousands of them at a time, and waited for the phone to ring. Our pricing structure was unique and had a history of driving sales.

Not so much this time. It was quiet. A couple of listings trickled in over the following months. I think I had two at a time once, but when you are charging a flat rate of $2,998–$4,998 depending on home value, that doesn't go very far. I spent upward of $40k on marketing in six months and closed five deals, recouping a grand total of less than

$20k of my initial investment. It was a failure, in every sense of the word.

Everything I had done in 2018, every endeavor, was a complete failure. I tried to do three very different, very far-apart things, all at once. This led to doing a piss-poor job at all of them. By September 2018, basically the day the first deal on the Manhattan house fell through, I knew I was in trouble. I was blowing through money on real estate marketing, had a $3k mortgage payment, and had the expenses of a growing family. And I was accustomed to making well in excess of $150k a year. To pour more gas on this fucking dumpster fire of a situation, which I alone created for myself, I decided to purchase a rental property in Townsend, a little town thirty minutes from Helena. It wasn't expensive, $90k, so I made a down payment of $20k, and it was a good investment, but it further dwindled my cash reserves. Looking back on this whole situation still leaves me confused as to what I was thinking. I must have been in complete denial about the reality of the situation to make some of the decisions I made during that year.

I was just throwing shit at the wall to see what might stick. I took on a house-flipping project too. All in, it took a month of my labor; I did new flooring and carpet, new light fixtures, new bathroom vanities, tile, paint, a sidewalk, and more. I invested tens of thousands into renovating the property. I finished around the end of October and listed it for sale. I hoped to make around $40k, but the market had other plans. It stayed on the market until December, and I accepted an offer that put $6k in my pocket. I would have made more just working for someone as a carpenter with my skill set.

I was panicked; I was nearly out of money by this time. I had started the year with more than $150k, and now I was sitting on less than $10k, or about one month's expenses, and $20k in credit card debt. I had basically no income, besides the roughly $800 a month from rental properties. I was functionally bankrupt. I was still waiting for the Manhattan house to close in early January. I had no listings or real estate clients at all. I went into survival mode; I listed all my rental property for sale, and then I did the unthinkable: I got a desk job. I had never thought I would work for someone ever again.

I was so afraid of going back to construction that I took a job for $25 an hour, plus commissions, at a manufactured home sales company. I was told that making $100k a year was probable after commissions. It wasn't. I realized it wasn't even possible once I saw the sales numbers of the branch I was hired to manage. I felt hopeless. I had a nice big office, and I should've been happy, right? I mean at least I wasn't a lowly construction worker anymore; I was the sales manager of a failing branch, at a dated company, making half the amount of money I needed to survive. Hooray!

I sat in that office from the week before Thanksgiving until just before Christmas. I was the most miserable I had ever been in my life. It was the most boring job on earth. Nobody ever came to look at the homes. That was the only lead generation to speak of, and any ideas I had about marketing were shot down. Days would go by when I wouldn't speak to a single customer. Just me and the other salesperson, Becky, sitting in the office with nothing to do, for weeks on end. I couldn't even use the computer in my office because it was such a piece of shit. Nobody cared. I wasn't even taking home enough money to cover my housing costs. I had to do something different.

I had finally come full circle. I had gotten burned out on doing construction labor, so bad that I left a six-figure job behind and the company that I had helped build. But now here I was barely a year later, having run through $150k in savings, depressed, anxious, out of shape, drinking a six pack or more a night, working some worthless fucking job that was going nowhere. I wasn't adding value to that company, or my own life. I felt like a failure in my wife's eyes. She never said as much, but how could she not see me that way? How could anyone who knew even the half of it not think it?

I had an epiphany one day. It just became so crystal clear: *What the* fuck *am I doing? I'm sitting here more miserable than I ever was working on a jobsite, making no money, when I could go do one siding project and take home more in a week than I have been in a month at the office.* At that moment right there in that soul-sucking office, I took decisive action. I Googled "builders in Helena Mt" and cold-called the whole list. I landed some opportunities to bid on projects from a couple of them, and Silver Creek Exteriors was born. By Christmas, I was doing my first project. I began to steer my life back on course, one siding project at a time. I quickly developed a good reputation and soon landed some reputable and consistent clients. I hired some help and just pressed on the gas as hard as I could, trying to put as much distance between me and the fucked-up situation I had created for myself as I could.

Had the rental properties not sold quickly and the spec house not closed on time and everything hadn't fallen together somewhat well, I would surely have lost everything. I was sinking fast. I would have gone from functionally bankrupt to destitute and losing my home in a couple more months. It cost me significantly selling those properties, as just a couple of years later they would be worth 30–40 percent more than what I sold them for, but it was the only option.

That was a long-winded story, but it serves to illustrate the danger of not recognizing this issue right away and having a plan to deal with it. All this hardship and turmoil for me and my family could've been avoided if I had just known how to recognize and deal with burnout before it got so bad that I couldn't keep going. Instead, I just powered through the feeling for years, not making any small changes or mindset alterations, and it festered and eventually caused a financial and personal catastrophe. A less crafty and determined man would've lost everything, yet a better, more mindful man would have never let it get that far. I strongly suggest learning to be the latter.

I will outline a few steps that I have since learned to cope with that feeling and keep moving in a positive direction. Because believe me, even when things are going well, it creeps back in, and often.

#1 SELF-REFLECTION

This is something that we should apply every day in every part of our lives. Look inward, and make sure that you understand your thoughts, feelings, actions, and the reasons you are experiencing them. Are you feeling burned out on work all together, or just this one project? Identify what it is that you are *actually* frustrated with, then you can take targeted action to mitigate the issues you are having with that particular part of your life. It's easy once you have trained that muscle a little; just take the problem and examine it from every angle in your mind—who is involved, what is going wrong, what is going right—and it will become evident quickly what the actual issue is when some conscious thought is applied. All too often we go through life and business being led by our emotions thinking that these feelings are what we *think*, but they are only what we *feel*. Don't allow your decisions to be made by emotion. Think through the situation carefully and wait until that initial gut reaction has passed before you make any decisions. That first reaction is just that—a reaction, a feeling. It's not thought out, it has no strategy or cleverness, it's just a feeling. Put it away while you make an adult decision based on the weighing of facts and circumstance.

Think of it like this: how many times have you felt like punching someone in the face? Ten, a hundred, ten thousand? Me too, but imagine what your life would look like if you acted on that every time. Not a pretty picture. The same goes for emotion surrounding work. If you always do what you feel like doing, you'll wind up bouncing from job to job, never getting ahead. Work on responding to situations, not reacting. Once you train yourself to think this way, you will spot that burnout feeling coming a mile away, giving you time to react in a constructive way.

#2 MAXIMIZATION

Learn to maximize the opportunity in front of you. It's not always sexy, but it keeps things interesting. Maybe it means you need to add a service to your business because you are bored with the same old thing every day, which can happen easily, as any tradesmen knows. You are doing the same goddamn thing every day, it all blends together, and when you have glued together your eight hundredth piece of PVC or driven your ten thousandth nail on the week, motivation and engagement can be pretty scarce and hard to muster. Adding an additional service can offer a little reprieve. Be intentional about what it is and how much you have to offer. Don't create a problem for yourself; make sure it fits in well with your current trade and it's something that you and your men already have the skills to execute.

Or maybe you need to adjust your attitude a little because you have gotten complacent. I have found the simplest and most effective course correction for me is to just focus on maximizing what I already have. It gives me new energy every time, and it's a 100 percent positive return. When I get bored or frustrated, I double down on making things more efficient, working faster, doing work of better quality, leaving cleaner worksites, servicing more clients, or whatever. I have made a habit of taking that feeling of boredom and burnout and using it as a call to action instead of a reason to retreat. Doing this alone will get you through those episodes of burnout, before they even begin. Unless you are already perfect at your job, which you're not—no one is—you have room for 0.1 percent improvement every day.

#3 CHANGING IT UP

On a crew, it's common for each person to have a designated job. On our siding crews, it's generally one cut man and two installers. They do those jobs every day. The cut guy cuts, and the installer installs, every day. It's great because everyone becomes hyper efficient at their craft. On the other hand, it adds to the monotony of the work. You begin to hate certain parts of your task so much that you start to avoid it and become inefficient, working around little inconveniences and annoyances until they pile up and shut production down altogether.

Sometimes it makes sense for everyone to switch jobs, but don't do this when the schedule is on the line and you need to perform at your team's full potential. But if you have even a little slack, that's a good time to implement this process. It's positive for two reasons: everyone gets a break from their designated job and gets a little extra brain stimulation breaking up the monotony, and it makes your team far more dynamic and capable when everyone can play every position. This way, if anyone is out for a day or for a week, or someone leaves altogether, the team can fill their shoes without much trouble. This can be done in short bursts or over longer periods. I find that starting short, like one day at a time, is the way to go, easing people into new roles, then over time as everyone becomes more efficient at each part of the job, you can stretch it out over longer periods of time, which is where it becomes a valuable tool for managing burnout within the ranks. Getting to do different parts of a job for several months at a time keeps things from getting painfully mundane.

#4 DAILY GOALS

This one ties in with the maximization I talked about earlier. Setting daily goals goes hand in hand with the maximization of what you are already doing. We know the overall goal is to complete each and every project as quickly and proficiently as possible while maintaining your standard and producing replicable results for your customers. This principle on its own lends itself to burnout; you may be on a project that lasts three days or thirty or three hundred. The three-day project is easy to stay motivated on; it's like a simple story arc, with a beginning, middle, and end. The thirty-day or three hundred–day project, not so much; you get lost in it, day in day out, the same location, the same issues, the same obnoxious superintendent or general contractor, and all the idiosyncrasies that come with them. By setting a daily goal, you create a road map for the project; you can feel the sense of accomplishment that comes with finishing what you set out to do every day.

I often break it down even further into before lunch and after lunch. I will be clear in my expectations with my crew; even now, although I don't work on the jobsite much anymore, I will swing by and set some goals for each team a couple of times a week, to encourage the team leader to do the same when I am not around. State what you expect to get done by lunch, and then after lunch. At first this can be difficult when the crew is new and you're not sure of the pace everyone is capable of, but over time you will get much more accurate with the time projections, and this will lead to a large increase in productivity in the long run.

For managing burnout, daily goals are a powerful weapon. A key component of this tactic is that the daily goal is set at the end of the prior day. This ensures that you don't adjust the goal based on how you feel in the morning. You will set more ambitious goals at the end of a successful day than you will bleary eyed and tired at 7 a.m. Setting goals aggressive enough that they are not always reached is equally important—in every area of life, not just on your jobsite. If you set easily obtainable goals every day, this exercise loses potency; it doesn't produce exciting results, and you slip back into monotony. On the other hand, if you reach your stated goal only 50 percent of the time, almost reach it 30 percent, and just flat out get your ass kicked 20 percent of the time, it keeps things interesting, because nobody—not you, not your lead, not the lowest-paid laborer on the team—wants to fall short on a goal. As men, as humans, we are hard wired to want to win at everything. We revel in success no matter how small, especially when the victory is hard earned. This is a basic principle for creating momentum as a team.

One of the great advantages we as tradesmen have over our white-collar peers is that we have the privilege of knowing without a doubt what we accomplish every day. The white-collar worker might work a ten-hour day behind his or her computer and put forth full effort but at the end of the day not really be able to tell you exactly what they accomplished. Even when they can, it's rarely tangible; they are often the only ones who know they had a productive day. Seldom do they get to trot their accomplishments out for others to see. Maybe they do when they close a deal or finish a project, sure, but day to day, the progress is hard to quantify. As a tradesman, you can see your progress, touch it, and feel it in your muscles and joints. Everyone else can see as well. You can take pride in your work and show people what you have done, and they can comprehend it easily; it requires no explanation when someone was staring at a blank wall of building wrap and by the end of the day it was covered in siding. Or when suddenly the power is back on in their office building, they know, and you know what was accomplished. The work is definite, so setting definitive goals and milestones on a daily basis is quite simple and highly effective in many ways, particularly in managing burnout.

To sum up these strategies, if you are getting burned out or worried about getting burned out, don't blow up your business or your job because you tried to pretend it wasn't happening. I see it often: someone just can't take it anymore, and they try something completely different, usually with problematic results. As you read above, I have done it myself. Instead of changing course or jumping off the boat, just look at the map and chart some new points. You started this journey for a reason. It's not the wrong journey; you just need a slightly different heading. Lastly, the enemy of burnout is progress. Track your progress in some way. It's easy to feel like you are stuck, but if you are making note of your wins and moving the needle toward your goals, it can inspire you to carry on day in and day out. The winners in business and life are not necessarily better than the losers; they are just the ones who kept moving forward, regardless of emotion or circumstance.

CHAPTER 11

HIRING AND RETAINING EMPLOYEES

This can be one of the most fucking frustrating and demoralizing parts of your job as a business owner, but it also has the potential to be the most rewarding.

I would like to say it's all up to you, but in truth, it's not. Sometimes you can be a great manager, be a good leader, and have installed good culture, but you still get some lemons. Sadly, with all the stigma around being a construction worker, we often get low-level, low-performing people who apply for these jobs. Sometimes it's out of your hands, but that in no way absolves you from the responsibility to be the best leader and employer you can be.

A large part of the issue stems from the general culture that tends to exist in the blue-collar trades and construction industry. Often, employers are jaded after years of dealing with parolees and general lowlifes, subsequently treating every new employee with the same kind of disrespect and vitriol they are accustomed to receiving as well as handing out. Many a talented young man has left a company, or the trades altogether, simply because of bad experiences with an employer.

Don't let that be you. I'm starting to sound like a broken record, but the keys to hiring and retaining quality employees are—you guessed it—clear communication and accountability.

Day one, you must set your standards and expectations by clearly communicating what those are and demand accountability to those standards every day from everyone, including yourself.

It is vitally important to create a culture around accountability to the work, to the team, and to the success of the team as a whole. If you can successfully implement this kind of culture from the first employee forward, your team will be easy to manage and will in many cases self-regulate. Your men will show up on time, work hard, and care about their work because each is accountable to the man next to him, not just to you or the check you are going to cut them. Under no circumstance can you allow one or more individuals to fail to be accountable or bring a shitty attitude to the workplace. If you allow this even temporarily, it will infect every member of the team. It may manifest differently in different people. Some will follow the bad apple down the tubes. Others will shift into neutral because they know they aren't in the spotlight; they are not the best or the worst employee, easily forgotten in the day-to-day. Your highest-performing people will become resentful at the situation that you are allowing to proliferate. Your inability or unwillingness to deal with the problem, to identify the cancer and cut it out, is creating a difficult situation for them to operate at the level they want to and at which you need them to. They will jump ship if you allow this type of thing to go on too long.

Although as many of us found in the early days post-COVID, employees have been hard to find, and they still are. There was a time when you just had to hire whoever walked through the door to try to keep your labor force intact. They were seldom good, almost never great. They brought bad attitudes and poor workmanship.

My best advice on this topic is to focus your energy on the good eggs and disregard the bad. Don't pour yourself and your limited resources into someone or multiple someones who are not going to give you a return on investment. Focus your attention on the best people, and craft them into the leaders and employees you want. They will in turn help train people the way you want them to be trained and move the company forward.

The sooner you can identify each type of employee, the better. It usually takes a couple of weeks to really see what someone is made of; almost nobody is late or no-shows the first week or two they work with you, but by week three or four, you usually get a glimpse of the future. Many men start to get complacent, showing up late, calling in with nonsense excuses. If it starts to spiral into that, there is no coming back, in my experience. Don't waste your time trying to see what their issue is and how you could help; simply warn them a couple of times and then cut them loose. Your effective and productive employees will thank you.

This is a short chapter because it's pretty simple: be respectful and demand respect; be accountable and demand accountability. Build the team you want, and don't let any losers drag you and your quality men into their low-standard way of life. You don't have time for it.

CHAPTER 12

LIFESTYLE CHOICES

This applies to every industry, though I think it plagues us blue-collar guys more than anyone. Society tells us that when you get done working your shift at the factory, the farm, or on the jobsite, the only logical thing to do is to head to the local watering hole and knock back half a dozen beers before you go see the family, and millions of blue-collar workers do just that, every day.

Every advertisement for cigarettes, chewing tobacco, and alcohol is leveled directly at blue-collar individuals. It has become a way of life for a lot of people rather than just a habit or a little bit of recreation. They start young going to the bar with all their coworkers, which is all well and good when they're twenty-one and single. But then twenty years go by, and they are still doing the same shit, spending two or three hours at the bar after work while the wife and kids are waiting at home, then driving home DUI drunk every night. That sure paints a nice picture, doesn't it? It's perpetuated by society too, in media and entertainment. Country music is the worst offender; its main subject matter is work hard, get drunk, repeat, with a catchy tune, so every dumb fuck from here to Arkansas can legitimize his terrible life choices through song.

It's an important thing to realize early on in your career in any blue-collar industry, because many of the men around you who are otherwise great guys and good mentors in your trade will be making bad lifestyle choices, and it will hold them back. Sadly, those guys are like crabs in a bucket—if you start to climb out, they will do their best to pull you back down, because they don't want to be a piece of shit by themselves.

Alcohol never made anything or anyone better. The culture built around alcohol is a parasitic relationship between a producer and a consumer; everyone loves it and legitimizes it while it infects society with all manner of maladies. The culture that tends to exist in the blue-collar workforce is a perfect host for this parasite. There is comradery built throughout the day that people wish to continue after work, and many people are already partaking in the nightly bar ritual. Then there are football games to watch and barbeques to attend, and pretty soon you and every man on your crew are drinking in excess almost every day. Sprinkle in positive reinforcement behavior by the media and entertainment industry, and you have a problem. Pretty soon, you are bringing beers to the jobsite. We have all seen it, beer in the trash cans at work—even guys who are just openly drinking while they work. There is not a single general contractor or client who is ok with that. They may tolerate it temporarily to get their project done, but they will be looking to replace you or ask you not to send that crew to their projects anymore.

The same goes for marijuana; it's a widely used substance in the construction industry, and it's now legal in many states. But under no circumstances should you or anyone on your crew be permitted to use it while at work. Again, we have all seen it, smelled it as we walked by the job trailer or whatever. There is always some asshat who says, "I need it, man. It makes me better at my job." No, it doesn't. I know firsthand, because in my early twenties, I was that asshat, and I was wrong. How could it make you better at your job than a clear, crisp, sober mind?

Now to be fair, I drink alcohol, have for my entire adult life, and will continue to do so. I'm not saying you can't partake in some of these things and still run a successful business. You can, yet you must be aware of when it's ok and how much is too much. I used to party pretty hard when I was single. I would be at the bar every weekend, drinking until I was shit-faced. Then on the weekdays I put away a six pack or more every night. I still managed to progress in my life and enjoy some success, but I know it held me back significantly. A key component here was that I never let it interfere with my work, at least directly. I would show up on time no matter what, and I was careful not to grossly overindulge on the weeknights, so that I would be serviceable at work. I'll admit I wasn't always my best, but I was able to perform. I set rules around drinking. It was never ok to drink at work, be drunk at work, or miss work because you were hungover, and that was it; otherwise, alcohol pretty much had its way with me for a long time. I struggled to control my drinking for more than a decade. I sometimes mourn the time I lost to alcohol. I would have been much further down the path without it. Now I have changed my relationship with alcohol completely. Now I am in control of it; I can have a beer or not have one, and I can stop after starting. I still enjoy drinks, and often, but I can confidently say it's no longer a factor in holding me back. Be sure you can say the same.

Abstaining from or at least controlling your drinking and drug use is an important part of having a successful career in any field, but it gives you even more of an edge in the blue-collar industries, because many people are not controlling it; it is controlling them. It's so widely accepted in the blue-collar space that it's hard for many of us to see the damage it's doing.

The same goes for physical fitness and diet. I know it sounds silly, but it's true. Who do you think has more energy for the workday and performs at a higher level and longer in their career? The overweight, out-of-shape guy with high blood pressure who has fueled his body with gas-station corn dogs and Mountain Dew, or the guy who has stayed in shape, gone to the gym, and made decent dietary choices? We all know what a stereotypical construction worker looks like. He is unkempt, is probably a little overweight, smokes cigarettes, drinks too much, has leather skin from the sun, looks fifty when he is thirty-five. There is no reason to be that guy. You can eat a healthy diet, exercise, limit your drinking, and definitely avoid smoking—it's terrible for you, you smell, and it is just generally unprofessional.

A lot of this lifestyle chapter boils down to rising above certain stereotypes. People expect you to look and act a certain way as a contractor or construction worker. They expect you to be dressed poorly, be generally unprofessional, smell like cigarettes, and be less than eloquent. If you show up to bid a job or have a meeting with a general contractor, and you are clean, look healthy, don't smell like an ashtray with liquor spilled in it, and can form a complete and grammatically correct sentence, you immediately change their perspective of you, and they will be far more likely to see you in a more professional, favorable way. There is no dress code in this industry, and nobody expects you in business attire, but you should consider who you are speaking with or meeting with and what their personal expectations may be.

Many tradesmen neglect to see the fact that the men and women who are the gatekeepers in the construction industry, the ones who have the contracts to award and checks to write, are often multimillionaires or decamillionaires. They go to fancy parties and charity events and drive expensive cars, live in big houses, and are friends with intelligent, well-spoken people; they will respond far better to a clean-cut, articulate individual than one dressed like a hobo who sends them misspelled emails or text messages.

All these things are choices. It's not "who you are" to be a dirty, chain-smoking redneck who would fail a third-grade spelling test; it's a choice you are making. If you want to be taken seriously by serious people, you must adapt a little bit.

I know firsthand that a lot of our jobs as tradesmen are dirty, and nobody will fault you at all for being a mess during the workday, but if you cut out time for a meeting or are out and about on the weekend, clean up, even if that means putting on a clean sweatshirt and washing your face and hands.

When you send an email, use the spell check tool that is literally on every device on earth at this point. When I get a text from an employee or a contractor or anyone for that matter, and every other word is butchered—and it happens a lot—I immediately think less of that person, less of their ability to pay attention to details, and less of the pride they will take in their work. I mean fuck, they couldn't even take the time to correct all the little red lines on the screen before they sent the message, so why should I believe they will do what is necessary to execute on the project they are hoping to be awarded or the job they are hired to do? I'm not some Ivy League fuck face who likes to correct people's grammar on the internet either; it is just something that everyone should be aware of when they are communicating with clients, customers, and employers.

The same goes for your personal appearance. Just try, even a little. Throw out the work shirt with ten holes in it, don't wear that pair of jeans that the ass is ripped out of so I can see your underwear, keep your face shaved or your beard trimmed, clean your truck out, and wash it once a week so you aren't driving around in a dumpster. Simple things go a long way in projecting the image you wish to have received of your company.

Who do you think has a better chance of being awarded a contract for $5k, $50k, or $500k—a guy who wore a Seahawks jersey with paint on it to a meeting, or someone who showed up in a clean, company-branded hat and sweatshirt?

You are the face of your business; present yourself accordingly.

CHAPTER 13

BUILDING A SCHEDULE

Building a schedule is easy; maintaining one is the challenge, especially in the construction industry. So much of the scheduling in construction is dependent on other trades that it can be nearly impossible to keep a schedule. It's a major headache for everyone involved. But as a subcontractor, you must be able to create a realistic schedule that puts you on time to projects and keeps work in front of your team every day. Having down time in your schedule is not good for revenue, and it's a bad look to your employees; they will look elsewhere for more reliable employment. On the other hand, having your schedule so full that you cannot service all the jobs and clients is not much better. This is an easy way to overload your team and burn them out, and your clients will look for other contractors because you are not executing for them. They have things to build, and your problem managing a calendar is not their issue, at least not for long. There is a low tolerance for showing up late to projects; make a habit out of it at your peril.

Many trades are what we call critical paths, meaning they need to be done before another trade gets started. A few are not, until they are, meaning it all must get done at some point before you hand the owner the keys, obviously. Although scheduling remains very important, there are less hard dates in trades such as siding, concrete flatwork, and exterior painting. You can move projects around with a little more flexibility, but my rule of thumb is to move a project only once; most generals are ok getting pushed back a week or two on one of these trades, but not a week two times.

If you are any of the other trades, the critical paths, your scheduling needs to be impeccable. You have a day or two of leeway tops, then people start getting frustrated. If you are a day behind, now so is every trade that comes after you. Below I'll outline a few strategies to mitigate scheduling issues. It's all basic; it just needs to be implemented.

#1 DON'T OVERCOMMIT

I always err on the side of caution with scheduling. I try to give myself conservative estimates on how long projects will take, and I always let my contractors know that the dates are tentative. They vary with weather and extenuating circumstances. I give a date range of a week when we are weeks away from starting, then a two-day window when we are about a week out; that gives me some wiggle room, and it keeps them apprised of where we are. It helps me often because it keeps them honest about whether the project is actually ready to start.

When you commit to the date, you will be there. You need to be there, period; just make it happen. This will ensure that they are ready for you every time, because they will learn quickly that you are for sure coming the day you said—not a week from then, but that day. If you have been intentional about how long things will take and built a conservative schedule around that, you will often be ahead of the game and be early to projects that are sitting waiting. This gives you enough margin to send the team home early on Friday now and then and not leave them without work on Monday.

It is so rare for a subcontractor to be on time to every project. It will instantly set you apart from your competition. It also makes scaling your business so much easier. Lots of construction businesses suffer the accordion effect. They start slow, don't have much work, then they take on a larger volume of work, they never say no to a project, they can't keep up, and they lose 75 percent of their clientele. Then they're slow again, hungry, and they take on too much work, over and over. When your scheduling is on point, you can make educated decisions about how many men you need on each team, how much work each team has in front of it, where the problem areas are, and which team needs to be on which project based on their pace of production.

#2 COMMUNICATE

Everyone in the construction industry knows that scheduling is a major logistical issue. It's not news; it's just part of the game. So if you communicate effectively with your clients, you will keep yourself out of hot water when it comes to scheduling. Let them know something has changed in your schedule, and see if they can work around it; chances are they can. Or you might learn that they have hit a delay and it actually works better that you are running behind, which happens surprisingly often. But don't assume, ask. If one client is in a bind, ask another if you can shuffle them back a week or whatever it is; if they are in a position to do so, they almost always will. If they can't, then you must figure it out on your own and honor the schedule you promised.

If you fuck up, and you will, and you find yourself in a bind such that you can't get somewhere when you said you would, you need to communicate that to the client who is getting burned as soon as you can, take full responsibility, and explain why this happened. Most guys are reasonable and have been there before themselves, so they will understand. Be clear and specific about when you will be there for real this time, and you'd better be right, because you don't get away with it twice.

In a worst-case scenario, you have fucked up your schedule so bad that you actually cannot get to all the jobs on it. Sometimes this happens because everyone gets their projects ready at the same time and it's not really your fault, but chances are, you did it to yourself. If this happens, you must swallow your pride and decide which client you would most prefer to completely fuck over, because that is the reality of this situation. It's that simple, and it's hard to do because someone gets screwed. You need to know that bailing on a project you already committed to is likely to end your relationship with that client, at least temporarily, because you are begging them to give their work to someone else; you're giving them no choice. Guess who they will hire the next time around. Pro tip: It's not you. You might get lucky and get them back at some point, but they will never be as loyal a customer as before you left them high and dry. In the event you are in this situation, and you likely will be at some point, pick the client you can do without or can most afford to lose; never do this to your main squeeze, thinking that your relationship is so solid that they will have your back. They might, but it will damage the trust between your two businesses permanently. Bottom line, this is a zero-star, would-not-recommend situation. Avoid it at all costs. Bring in a second-tier subcontractor, work by yourself on the weekend on their project, communicate to the client why and how it happened, and they will see how hard you tried to make things work for them. You might actually build some loyalty instead of losing it.

#3 KEEP TABS ON YOUR CLIENTS' PROJECTS

This one is easy to miss. You need to ensure that you know at approximately what stage of construction each project for every client is at all times. I do this once a week; I drive all around the valley just eyeballing houses that my clients are building. I take notes with addresses, stating the progress of each build. This allows you to build your schedule out further than just waiting for your client to call and tell you the project is ready, or it will be ready next week. Ready or ready next week mean different things to different people; go put eyes on it yourself, and you'll quickly develop a feel for the way each clients builds progress and be able to create accurate scheduling. I do it enough that I have a working understanding of how long it takes each crew that does frame construction for all our clients to build a standard house. I know crew 1 takes three weeks and crew 2 will take five or more weeks on the same project. I can plug that estimate into my schedule now, refining it further.

You should be able to have a conversation with your client and demonstrate a clear understanding of where each project is in production and what your schedule is looking like and confirm when they expect you at each one. This conversation will likely be had on a weekly basis and change every time. And each time, you should already have the information. You should sound like "Hey I saw X project is framed and waiting on the roofer; when do you anticipate the electrician will start that one?" You should not say, "How is X project coming? Is it ready?" See the difference? If nothing else, it gives the impression that you are on top of what is going on and ready to execute for your client.

In summary, scheduling is often the number-one headache for any kind of construction manager, so if you can effectively mitigate as many scheduling issues as you have control over, you will gain a massive advantage over your competitors and come out as a preferred subcontractor in your area because you are making every client's job easier.

CHAPTER 14

MAKING THE TRANSITION FROM FIELD TO OFFICE

There are more ways than one to become a white-collar tradesman. The primary focus of this book is the entrepreneurial route to that dream. Another very viable opportunity that can't go unmentioned is to become an intrapreneur at an existing company.

Not everyone is built for owning a business—like almost no one, statistically speaking. If you have been reading along and are thinking "fuck all this" or feel overwhelmed by the inherent unpredictability of owning a business, pay close attention to the next few pages. They are for you.

Currently, less than 10 percent of the adult American workforce is entrepreneurs; half of them fail in the first five years, and 7 percent or less of those businesses gross over $1 million per year. Less than 2 percent of business owners ever earn six figures themselves inside their business. It's not exactly a statistically viable career path, especially when you are setting your sights on a six-figure salary.

If you find yourself reading that dismal data and recoiling at the thought of working your ass off with statistically little chance of success, you are obviously not alone. It doesn't compute for most people, no matter how driven or high functioning they are. The intrapreneurship path is much more predictable and stable. Although it rarely offers a huge salary and has somewhat limited upward mobility, it's still a great opportunity to make a six-figure salary, work a normal schedule, and have the option to leave work at work, luxuries your business-operating counterparts do not have. If this more traditional path appeals to you, there are some steps that you need to be intentional about taking if you want to get into that corner office making phone calls and estimating projects instead of pounding nails forever.

SELECTING YOUR WAGON

First select a company based on research into its size, the type of work it does, the market share it has, if it's growing, and what the culture seems to be or is portrayed as. Ask some of the employees, if you can, what it's like to work there. You are selecting a wagon to hitch yourself to, and you are going to help pull this wagon; make sure you like it and it has what you want and need, because you are about to become intimately familiar with it and all its baggage, issues, and idiosyncrasies.

Do as deep a dive possible on several companies and select the one that you feel fits best for you. Once you have selected a company, now you must go get hired. This part shouldn't be hard. The trades are experiencing a massive shortage of workers and have been for twenty years. But don't take that for granted.

Many construction workers show up for an interview in the same clothes they will wear to the jobsite on Monday:

dirty, torn-up jeans with paint on them and a sweatshirt repping their favorite bar or sports team. Don't do that. You'll look like a loser, a go-nowhere, trailer-house-living, broken-down-truck-driving, fucking hillbilly. Even if you get hired, you will be typecast as that hillbilly from day one and will never have a chance to rise to that corner office you are after. No one will give you that chance.

You interviewed at this company because you want to work your way to a white-collar job, right? So show up for your interview dressed like a white-collar worker. The adage "dress for the job you want" couldn't be truer here. Don't go overboard and wear a three-piece suit and tie; you'll look like an ass. But put on a clean ironed pair of jeans or slacks and a button-down shirt—something, anything, that doesn't scream "I want to pound nails and sweep floors until I retire."

Show up with some questions written down that you would like to ask, bring a printed résumé, maybe a letter about yourself; show some preparation and thoroughness. Often, twenty minutes of research and preparation can make you come off like a savant compared with the next guy. It doesn't have to be perfect; you're not applying for a job in traditional corporate America, but still, do what you can to distance yourself in the employer's mind from the guy who showed up in a tattered sweatshirt smelling like cigarettes.

PROVE YOUR WORTH

So, you got the job at your selected company. Now what? Well, depending on where you are on your journey, the timeline to the corner office will be different, but the path is very much the same. One thing that needs to be made abundantly clear from the date you interview to the day it happens is that you intend on working at the company for a long time, and you want that corner office job.

Let's say it's your first day on a construction site, and you have your sights set on the corner office and a six-figure salary. Just like in any profession, this is going to take time, effort, and accountability to the process. You will start by learning the basics of your trade; this will take a minimum of one year, in my opinion. Within a year, you should be able to perform the duties of a plumber, carpenter, concrete finisher, or what have you, with little to no direction. You will have questions still and often, but you'll have the concepts committed to memory. I believe it takes a minimum of five years for someone to master a trade of any sort; that's if they are smart and work intentionally to do so. Though keep in mind that this leg of the journey isn't over.

Now you can start to build your general knowledge base with intention. You will have learned much through osmosis just being on the site and working around other trades and tradesmen. Now you can start applying yourself to learning more about how a jobsite runs, about what it looks like when things are going well and what it looks like when they are not. Pay special attention to the order of operations for the construction process, to what can be skipped over temporarily and what things are showstoppers. Learn how to read plans correctly and thoroughly. Do everything you can to be as on top of the process as possible. This will make you of far higher value than the "I just work here" guy. You might catch something the boss missed on the plans or answer someone's questions with certainty. You will start to stand out from the crowd, and you're beginning to prove your worth. Your foreman and managers will start to see you as an asset instead of just another warm body. This phase will likely last some time, as it takes time to learn the skills and knowledge necessary to run a job effectively.

Like I said earlier, it takes a minimum of five years to master a trade, and it takes equally as long to become an effective project manager or superintendent. I am saying that you can learn them both simultaneously instead of in succession. When I built my first spec home, I had received zero training of any kind in general contracting other than observation. Granted, there were a few mistakes, but overall, it was a resounding success—proof positive, anecdotal as it may be, that while learning to master a single trade, you can also learn the skills necessary to take the next step forward.

Now, you have learned your trade in one year, and the next four years were spent on mastery and fleshing out your skill set to become a well-rounded student of the construction industry. By now, you should be a foreman and have been for a while, running a team on the ground at the jobsite. Once you have reached that foreman or team lead position and proved you can execute on it for an extended period, then and only then will you even be in the running for that corner office job. A key component of this stage is that you need to be proactive in training someone on your team as your replacement. Your boss is not likely to promote his best foreman if no one can take his place; ensure you can confidently tell your boss that whomever you have groomed for the position is capable of doing the job. If you have discharged your duties with purpose, shown up to work every day, made improvements, and trained your replacement, you are ready to take the next step.

Next, simply go ask for the corner office. Your employer needs to know you aspire to this position. If you paid heed to the first paragraph of this chapter, you were clear about your intention to sit in the corner office early on, and frequently throughout the years. So it should come as no surprise that you are asking. If you have executed on your job and beyond for a period of five years and have provided value to the company you work for, there is no reason for them to say no other than that the position is currently filled or that you are too valuable where you are. Often, if you have chosen a company that wishes to invest in its people, your boss might have already been working toward creating a position in a corner office for you, as they recognize the need for someone like you to progress and they don't want to lose you to the guy up the road.

Whatever happens, you have built a war chest of skills and knowledge that will serve you for decades to come. You can take it with you wherever you go and always at least be in the running for the upper-level jobs. The rest is up to you.

Six-figure salaries are few and far between in the construction industry while working inside someone else's business, but they exist. If you want one, you must become undeniably good at your job. It's that simple. Become so effective that your boss has no choice but to pay you more just in hopes of keeping you in the fold. Produce undeniable results, and you will be compensated accordingly.

CHAPTER 15

SUMMARY

No matter what path you choose or what trade you enter, there is so much opportunity for success and growth in the trades. America is on the precipice of a second industrial revolution. Manufacturing, civil construction, residential construction, and commercial construction are going to explode, and we are already understaffed in those areas. The opportunity for high-performing people to make fortunes in this space of the economy has never been better. I know it can be difficult to take that first step toward something. Even just having the courage to go after that corner office position we talked about can be daunting. It's hard to believe in yourself, especially when all your life the media and people around you have told you that being a tradesman or a construction worker or a factory worker or whatever is a less-than-desirable path. People and culture have tried to typecast you as someone who stays where they are and struggles to get by, and you believe them; hell, even I believed them for a time.

Open your fucking eyes and see that it's a lie. Look at the guys who are winning in this space. There are more of them every day. Guys are making millions of dollars and started out as carpenters and plumbers. I know half a dozen guys my age who are sitting on over a million dollars in their *bank account*, not even counting the assets they have. These guys are HVAC contractors, plumbers, and electricians who still wear their tool bags most days and crawl around on their knees in a dusty crawl space or sweat it out in the summer heat, just like you are now. They have just applied the principles we talk about in this book, and they have risen above a foolish stereotype.

Remember, the point of this book was to get you—yeah, *you*—to garner the courage to take that first step across the bridge. I told you in the first chapter of this book that there was a bridge from where you are, pounding nails, taping drywall, digging ditches, or nailing shingles for wages, to where I am, to providing quality jobs, solving industry problems, and making a salary that would make your average architect, lawyer, or doctor blush with embarrassment at their own paycheck.

I have no special skills, no special talents, and I'm not exceptional in any way other than the fact that I can execute consistently and have learned a lot of things to do and not to do over the course of almost two decades in the trades. I gave you everything that I have to offer in this book, and I have a surplus of empirical evidence that when the concepts and principles discussed in this book are applied with urgency, discipline, purpose, and patience, they will create a desirable result. It may be less than what I have achieved, or it may be considerably more impressive, but like I said, I am just here to help you take the first steps, to cross the bridge from a burned-out, disenfranchised wage earner to a man with direction and purpose in his career who can help others along the way. The rest is fully up to you and the effort you are willing to apply and the sacrifices you are willing to make.

This book is not just a how-to guide, but also a call to action. Stop living below your potential. Stop letting your family live a life that is less than what you are capable of providing. Gather the courage to take your first steps, and you will see the path unfold before you and that a boundless opportunity awaits. I implore you to go out and achieve at a higher level than you are, to create jobs and opportunities for other men in your community, and to help build the future of America.

ABOUT THE AUTHOR

Brock J. Gebhardt, a seasoned professional with two decades in the construction industry, shares his wealth of knowledge in Becoming a White Collar Tradesman. His experience spans nine years of self-employment and over five years managing a business with employees. A former real estate agent and investor, Gebhardt is driven by the desire to guide young individuals towards lucrative opportunities in the trades. He draws inspiration from his personal life, balancing his career with raising two children and maintaining a small farm in Helena, MT. His book aims to bridge the gap between young job seekers and the thriving construction industry.